In Search of the Creator

A DOCTRINE OF PEACE AND UNDERSTANDING

Rabbi Michael J Eljarrat

The copyright holder can be contacted:
By e-mail eljarrat@mweb.co.za
Telephone 00 27 11 485 1731

Cover Picture: Michael J Eljarrat –Image Monikandra©
A picture summary of the contents of this work
Managing Editor: Bruce Douglas
Written by: Michael J Eljarrat

CONTENTS

This book is dedicated

To my precious daughter Sofia Zahava, it should be the will of Hashem, that you have strength and wisdom all the days of your life.

You have entered a world bereft of human kindness; Love those who love Hashem, and you will never be disappointed.

Choose to be a good person; always think before you act. When Hashem is with you, you will never fail. Call to Hashem in truth, and he will answer.

My love for you is eternal and unwavering. Go forward with strength, as the light of the sun.

Be your true self, be who that you really are.

Serve Hashem and become a better person each day.

FORWARD

Over the past number of years, we have been witness to a great number of changes in our world, some positive and some otherwise. At the core is a sense that civilization is moving backwards rather than forward, as we see the spiritual holocaust of the past manifesting again in the present. There is an ever growing need to return back to the basics and reestablish our humanity.

There is one thing we can see with certainty though, and that is, history repeats itself. As we examine the rise and fall of various empires, an unmistakable pattern emerges, namely humility and kindness build, whilst arrogance and selfishness destroy. When leaders have forgotten what their ancestors fought for, and have become bloated with power, decline is almost an inevitable outcome.

For those who are alert and spiritually awake, it is clear to see that we are in decline. When Democracy was lost in ancient Greece, it did not reappear for centuries. For those that choose to ignore the global situation, major change will come as a huge surprise.

In Search of the Creator is a call to humanity, a call to curtail the current holocaust, and the era of destruction which we are presently living through. It beckons to humanity, to return to good and truth.

What this book aims to achieve is, a deeper understanding for all humanity, to build rather than to destroy. Every human being has a unique role to play in the history of the world. Collaboration rather than competition will enable the human race to achieve the maturity it so desperately needs.

In Search of The Creator seeks to show the reader that as human beings we have more in common than we have in differences. In a world where love and compassion have been lost, this text seeks to revive an age old message, the message of acceptance and tolerance, spoken but ignored countless times throughout history.

By understanding the universal truths, we can remove the clutter, and find our way back to both inner and outer peace.

This text incorporates the discussion, around many issues that have divided the human race. It touches upon some sensitive topics which have remained mute for decades. By asking questions rather than providing answers, the reader will be challenged to seek clarity.

> ഗ്ര
> We are all just human beings in search of the Creator.
> ഗ്ര

With this in mind I have tried to bridge the cultural divides, and bring home the message that we are all just human beings in search of the Creator.

Please note that this book is intended for study purposes, rather than reading.

Structural errors in syntax are purposeful, to guide the reader in post formal thought and dialectical thinking as proposed by Kallio (2012). In order to preserve the emotional content and authenticity of the message, only minor editing has been applied. For further reading see: Everyday Creativity in Language: Textuality, Contextually, and Critique Applied Linguistics (2007) 28 (4): 497-517 Janet Maybin and Joan Swann.

A MESSAGE FROM THE EDITOR

For more than seven years, Bruce Douglas has worked in the fields of community and online journalism. An award-winning reporter, Bruce also runs a digital blog for the Newcastle Advertiser. A staunch supporter of the written word, Bruce is in the process of final copy-editing for his debut novel.

Knowledge is power.

I have steered my life by this statement, seeking to know more every day, to gain wisdom through constant challenging of my mind. Reading is a fundament of learning.

Thus, when Rabbi Michael asked me to revise his book, the first step I took was to learn from its pages and empower myself.

I consider myself more enlightened from his words. His brand of Soul-Chology is self-explanatory; taking knowledge from In Search of the Creator is undergoing psychology from the base outwards.

It is more than a simple book - it is a guide. If you have been lost while looking for the Creator, Rabbi Michael has compiled a work more valuable than a map.

There is practical wisdom in these pages. Predominantly esoteric in nature, this book provides an informative and comprehensive path for seekers and believers alike.

Books and words are meant to be used. Take what you can from In Search of the Creator, gain understanding of our united goal to live in service of the Creator and let it shape you.

Knowledge is a tool which can change the world. You might think this statement a bit cliché, although my belief is that humanity could benefit from more information, more awareness of our actions.

Read with an open mind and read often. When I become a father one day, my legacy if anything, will be to gift my children with the might of the written word, and to always know more. Knowledge is power - we are the conduits.

Bruce Douglas

PREFACE

As The Cerebral Type, I have always had impossible dreams that I call goals. My goal was and still is, to talk face to face with the Creator of the universe.

The first lesson that I learnt was, having a pure heart, or being emotionally compelled to seek the Creator, is more important than intellectual ability.

I have experienced almost every misfortune and heartache known to man, chasing my ridiculous dream. But my dream is still alive, and I see every misfortune, as a way for the Creator to humble my soul and ready me for the experience that I yearn for.

The pre-requisite for finding benefit in my writings is an open-mind and a pure heart. Through this method you will no doubt obtain:

1. A still mind.
2. Clear thoughts.
3. A strong soul.

Those who have experienced the realm of spirituality will undoubtedly know that, in the current state of world affairs, clinging to the Creator requires incredible strength of character.

The life of the atheist may seem tolerable for now, but when the existential crisis begins, the atheist too will be searching for the Creator.

I hope to make an impact on future generations, who will once again yearn for meaning. I resolved within myself to write, not for personal gain, but for the good of humanity, to alleviate the suffering of those enduring this spiritual holocaust.

Let me state clearly: There is a single Creator of all, do not doubt that you have a soul, do not doubt the ability of the Creator, and do not be misled by anything which reduces you to nothing more than a "meat machine".

I will share my struggle with you, and remind you that you are a proud human being; your essence is your soul, a part of the Creator. Although the Creator is in tremendous hiding, in reality the Creator is hiding in plain sight.

There are two types of individuals:

1. The conformist, who has become lost in the rituals of their religion, and who emulate man.
2. The courageous, those who use all their ability, to do right in the eyes of the Creator, despite the incredible ridicule that this entails.

I never imagined that, I would live through a time, where using knowledge for pure evil would be a quality, and a virtue to strive for. I did not envisage a world, so void of spirituality, with the word of the Creator being reduced to "practical" ritual, as if to deny the Creator himself. The souls of the human race are emaciated.

If what I have said above resonates with you, you are among the righteous.

The Creator can be found in two places:

1. The first is, as an abstract concept.
2. The second is, within the creative spirit of the human being.

When the Temple stood the presence of the Creator could be felt strongly. This manifested in two ways firstly the abstract concept of the Creator seemed less abstract, and more tangible; secondly the creative spirit among people was stronger.

Now that the Temple has been destroyed, the Creator is more abstract and distant, and people have less creative spirit.

Creative spirit in the human being does not necessarily refer to art or music or other constructs which come to mind, but rather what I call character.

Creative spirit or character means being bold and having passion. People with character don't do things in half measure; they are confident in their ways and exhibit themselves fully.

One cannot purchase uniqueness or a pure heart

Those with character pride themselves on being different, within the fundamental substance of their personality. They possess virtue and integrity.

Unfortunately today we have lost our privacy and uniqueness. We have also lost our communities, our group of people traveling through the journey of life together, like a large extended family.

Communities are formed when likeminded individuals congregate in a particular location based on a shared sense of purpose. It has been painful to watch, the collapse and wilful destruction of our communities.

Growing up, I was fortunate enough to have had a community, and one could display acts of loving kindness without fear of reprisal. It was even acceptable to be kind-hearted.

The Creator can only be found in that which is unique, and pure hearted. One cannot purchase uniqueness or a pure heart, and thus we have drifted far away from our source.

As it is written:

"For this commandment, that I command you today. - It is not hidden from you and it is not distant. It is not in heaven for you to say, who can ascent to the heaven and get it for us, so that we can listen and perform it? Nor is it across the sea for you to say, who can cross the sea and take it for us, so that we can listen and perform it? Rather it is very close to you **in your mouth and in your heart - to perform it**."

Deuteronomy 30:11-14

1

THE SEARCH BEGINS

To all created beings of light energy, from all realms and dimensions, of our shared Multiverse; we were all brought into existence, for the service of our Creator.

Remember Source; Creator of all, and carry the weight of the responsibility as you have been tasked with.

The starting point:

Let me cut straight to the chase and answer a few questions which you may have.

Question: Where is the Creator?
Answer: Everywhere, and more specifically, inside of you is a direct link called a soul.

Question: How can I communicate with the Creator?
Answer: As a human being you have the power of speech. (Other species connect in different ways) The only way to communicate with the Creator is to speak the **truth** to the Creator. Speak out what you are feeling, and you are talking to the Creator, it's that simple!

Question: If I am already connected to the Creator then what is personal growth?
Answer: Growth means knowing yourself well, and becoming a unique individual. This entails self-control and character refinement.

Question: What does it mean to be unique?
Answer: Finding your true unadulterated self, and becoming the best possible version of you. (Remember the only thing that you cannot become is someone else!)

Question: How do I find my true self?
Answer: There is no single method; however you will need some time alone to become a master over your own thoughts.

Question: What is character refinement?
Answer: In a nutshell it is impulse control, i.e. your ability to think before you act, using your brain as a tool to control your body.

Let's begin.

Society has taught you that showing emotions is frowned upon, and so you have learnt to supress all your emotions and feelings. However you will need these emotions very shortly and I will show you how to unblock that "emotion drain".

Emotional pain is the body's way of telling you that something isn't right. This is great, because you already have everything you need to fix it.

The worst thing to do is to pretend that everything is ok, when it isn't. As I said above, the only way to connect with the Creator is with truth, this means sharing your pain. Any pretending is not truthful.

Your emotions are your greatest asset when it comes to connecting to the Creator. A heartless boring speech is not nearly as powerful as a cry from the bottom of your heart in total desperation.

The Creator wants your emotions, and if you have been suppressing them, you have unknowingly cut yourself off from the Creator.

Look at the diagram on the following page and see where you are currently at.

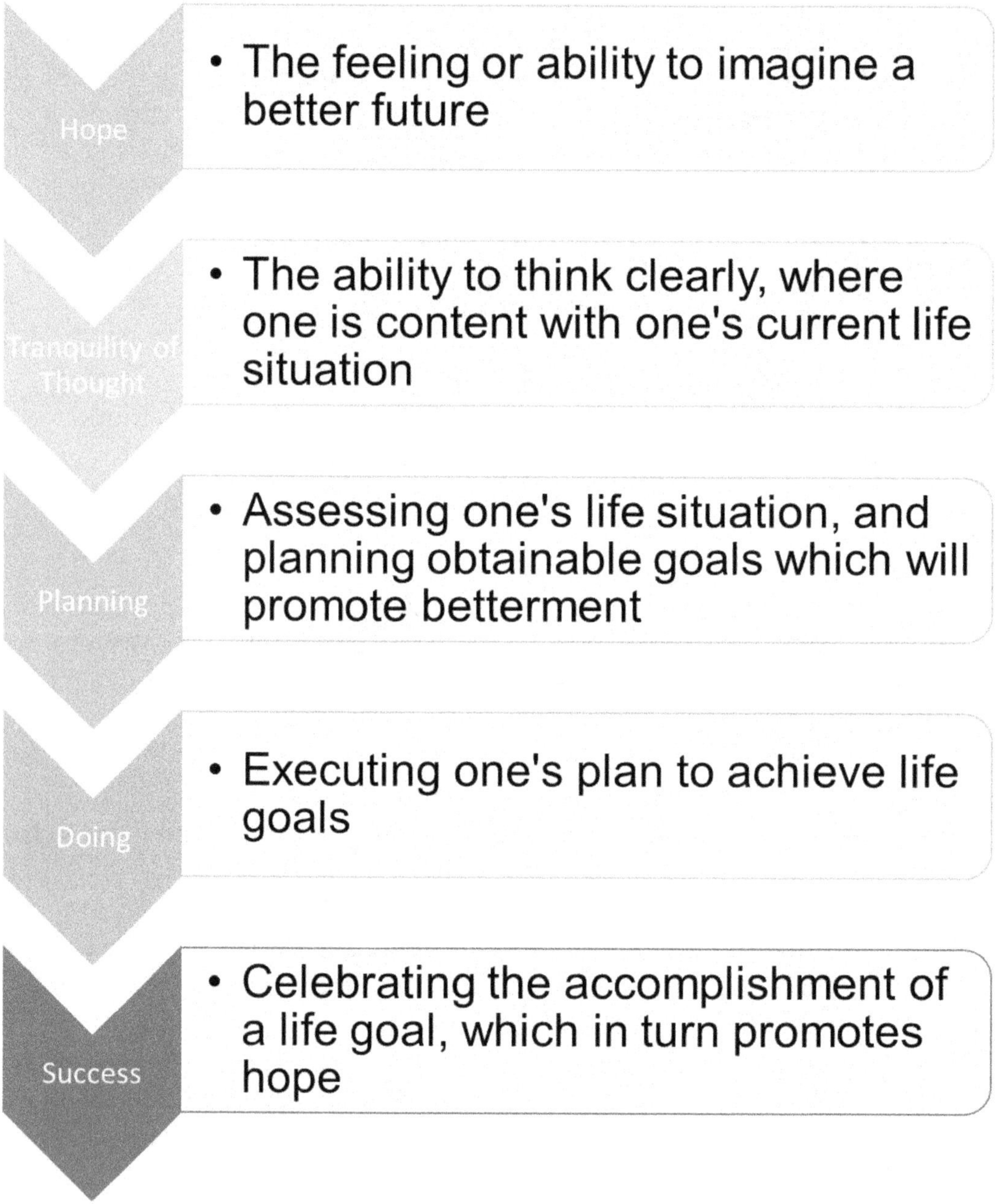

Hope

- The feeling or ability to imagine a better future

Tranquility of Thought

- The ability to think clearly, where one is content with one's current life situation

Planning

- Assessing one's life situation, and planning obtainable goals which will promote betterment

Doing

- Executing one's plan to achieve life goals

Success

- Celebrating the accomplishment of a life goal, which in turn promotes hope

As human beings we go through various cycles and stages in life. Each one of these stages brings about its own set of unique emotions. The emotions felt with each stage, create a unique opportunity to use the power of speech. By talking to the Creator at each of these life points, you can build a very unique relationship with the Creator.

Hope:
Many people meet the Creator at the junction between hope and hopelessness, so I will focus just on this stage.

The greatest asset which a human being can own is hope. Broadly speaking hope is the ability to imagine a better future:

It is easy to overlook the great power of hope. When a person has hope he/she does not appreciate the immense value that hope brings to their general wellbeing.
A person who is unable to envision a better future becomes hopeless. The prayers of the hopeless are very sweet in the eyes of the Creator, as the mere act of finding the energy to open one's mouth and break the silence is a tremendous feat.

Depression is the sickness of intelligent individuals, who have lost hope.

When a person is in a difficult predicament and has intelligence and foresight, it is very easy to lose hope. Depression is the sickness of intelligent individuals, who have lost hope.

Hope can be gained through a number of ways some of which include:

Success: When you achieve a desired goal and hence you feel wanted, needed and appreciated, you will automatically feel hopeful.

Positive social connections: A social environment which promotes your success. Being around people who want to see you succeed and who motivate you.

Positive attitude: Having a resilient mind-set of not giving up despite extreme adversity.

Purpose: Having a calling or a sense of purpose which lies beyond you.

Hope can be lost through a number of ways some of which include:

Failure: If you fail at attaining a life goal, and are unable to correct the failure, or find meaning in the suffering, hope is often lost.

Lack of social connection: When you have extreme isolation or a negative social environment, hope is eroded.

Abuse: If you are abused, tormented or undermined on a continuous basis, your self-esteem can be damaged which in turn can result in hopelessness.

In the harsh world that exists; where good people are trampled on and abused, and where dishonesty is a virtue, it is almost impossible not to lose hope.

Although some may mock and disgrace those who believe in the Creator, it is essential to know and understand that no human being can disprove the existence of the Creator, and therefore if belief in the Creator gives you hope, then it is absolutely essential to hold onto your hope and your faith. Own your faith proudly.

Individuals who have not suffered enough in life, and who have been given only privilege and unearned opportunity, are often oblivious to the entire concept of hope.

So what's next?

Up next is some hard work, sorry to disappoint you. But like anything worthwhile it takes a lot of effort and perseverance. No one can become great by accident, for some reason people often incorrectly assume that spiritual greatness can be bought or inherited or the like. Nothing can be further from the truth.

If you want to know the recipe I suggest that you study (not read) two books by the Ramchal[1]. Start with Derech Hashem (The way of God) to understand the mechanics of spirituality, and then move on to Mesilas Yesharim (The path of the just). This will give you a taste of what masters do, to become godlike in nature.

There's an old saying which goes; the best time to plant a tree was 20 years ago, the second best time is today.

Some of you may become masters and reach the twelfth level of greatness, and I'm sure you will. Even if you make it to the first set, I'm sure that you will find it rewarding.

Before you start the Ramchal's 12 step program, you need to be a "Yoshor" - A straight person.

Being a Yoshor means being level headed, rational, and honest. For some this is no big deal, for others it means digging deep into their soul and finding these qualities.

There are 5 qualities which you need to develop as a starting point.

1) Understanding the greatness of the Creator.
2) Acting like the Creator.
3) Loving the Creator and wanting to please the Creator.
4) Having pure intentions.
5) Performing all the duties of the Creator diligently.

In the chapters to follow, you will develop these 5 qualities and be well on your way to spiritual success.

The chapters ahead may seem difficult to read, take it slowly and try absorbing the content; the effort will be well worth it.

[1] Rabbi Moshe Chaim Luzzatto

2

THE CREATOR IS SIMPLE

The Creator is simple; man has made it complicated

I will attempt to unravel and un-complicate some of the core issues faced by humanity in this period. I will discuss those issues which cloud the mindset of the human race.

I will challenge some preconceived ideas, popular theories and beliefs, some of which are often nothing more than distractors, which throw us off our primary goal, of seeking wisdom and becoming something more.

I will examine this doctrine and source its origin. In the theory of change and perturbation, it is noteworthy to mention that our own frame of reference is often the greatest hindrance, to greater understanding.

"In an ingenious mental turnaround, Einstein turned this puzzle into a postulate! Instead of worrying, for the moment about how it could happen [The speed of light being 186,000 miles per second], he simply accepted the experimentally irrefutable fact that it does happen." (Zukav 1980 p135)[2]

[2] Family Therapy – A systemic Integration – Becvar and Becvar 2013, Pearson, New Jersey

Let us follow suit and just for the moment, let us accept the Creator, and then based on what is presented here, choose for yourself, to either accept or reject what is being proposed.

I have no desire to change others, not only because the only person I can influence is I, but because I strongly believe in individuality and personal freedom to choose.

Let me be the first to critique my own work as being incomplete. Understanding the human condition is a mammoth task, which requires careful deliberation over each of the many segments. My intention is to start a discourse on many concepts which need clarification, with the ultimate goal of providing a more peaceful planet for all who exist.

"Seven character traits are found in a wise person[3]

He/she does not speak before those greater than him/her-self.
He/she does not interrupt the words of another.
He/she does not answer carelessly.
He/she asks questions with relevance and replies accurately.
He/she speaks sequentially.
He/she says about something he/she has not heard "I have never heard it"
He/she admits to the truth.

The opposite is true of a fool"

I hope to be wise in seeking clarity and sharing my thoughts and ideas with all those who want to know and understand their Creator. I invite you, the reader, to journey with me on the road less travelled.

[3] Ovos 5:9

The point of departure for this work:

We will take on the premise that a Creator does in fact exist, and it is our goal to seek out the aforementioned Creator. Our second premise is that seeking the Creator will entail a journey of the mind, using our faculties of reason and questioning, as well as emotion.

There are numerous reasons why we will not depart from the atheist perspective. Some of these reasons include:

1. The vast arrays of atheist stand points, which vary in terms of the definition, spectrum and scope, as well as the reasoning behind these stand points; all of this will warrant an entirely separate work, systematically addressing each point of contention.

2. In the current period of world history, theism is a view held by the majority of the population.

3. Theism has existed for a longer period in world history, than has atheism.

4. The burden of proof may lie with the atheist; this would entail a deep study of the approximately 4200 religions of the world and their disproof, as well as an all-encompassing grand unified theory of everything.

5. By way of analogy, if one does not find aspirin in the hardware store, one cannot conclude that aspirin does not exist, but merely that one has looked in the wrong place. So too, if one does not look for spirituality using the appropriate methods, one cannot conclude that spiritual beings do not exist. Emotions such as love and hate are also difficult to prove, but we find consensus to their existence.

The second premise: seeking the Creator entails a journey of the mind:

World travel broadens the mind, and alleviates many of the cognitive biases which we will soon discuss. While it is true that those who have travelled extensively are vastly wiser than those who have not, the concept of seeking a non-physical entity in a physical location is flawed in its logic.

However, further on we will discuss the relationship between physicality and spirituality. It should soon become apparent to the reader that this "search" is one of understanding and wisdom, and not like any other conventional search.

We will now explore these statements in finer detail, but before we do, we must be aware that as human beings we are faced with a plethora of psychological biases, which obscure our insight and cloud our judgement.

Two psychological biases which are particularly harmful, are:

Recency effect – the tendency to weigh recent events more than earlier events (see also 'peak-end rule'). In general, we are biased in our thinking of current events, and as such, we tend to think that "Man" has reached his ultimate state of knowledge and understanding in this current period of time, as this is happening in the present.

This way of thinking excludes the possibility that man goes through historical periods of great knowledge, as well as periods of great regression in knowledge.

The popular belief is that mankind has progressed in a linear fashion with regards to his attainment of knowledge. Others postulate that mankind's knowledge has progressed in a step-like fashion, with periods of great discoveries followed by periods of leveling off and then followed by periods of even greater discoveries.

In reality, we have amassed a vast scientific knowledge today; although it has taken us many thousands of years to get to the point we find ourselves today.

In all likelihood it will take many thousands of years for us to progress to any profound holistic, complete body of scientific knowledge.

At best, we can say that we are currently in the "Stone Age" of the science which will prevail in 6000 years from now. Our scientists today are the "Cavemen" in the year 8018.

If one approaches spirituality from a purely scientific mindset, then atheists have solid ground to stand on; it would be impossible to use such primitive science to prove the existence of the Creator, much like it would be impossible to create a space shuttle using stone tools.

I would wholeheartedly agree with individuals such as Richard Dawkins for one reason only, namely the infancy of our current science. However, I would argue that science can in fact be used as a tool to understand our Creator. After all, intense study of the created will inevitably lead back to the Creator.

Perhaps, in 6000 years from now, assuming science and technology continues to develop, at its current rate, I believe that evidence of a Creator will be obtainable from every industry and from every academic field of study.

In addition, we cannot simply ignore the work of scientists such as Alfred Rupert Sheldrake, who brings to light many flaws of modern-day science, or the work of medical doctor Dr. Deepak Chopra, who maintains that consciousness is located outside of the human brain, nor the work of theoretical physicist, Roger Penrose and anesthesiologist, Stuart Hameroff who postulated that consciousness can be found within the brain. Nor can we ignore the work of researcher Robert Allan Monroe who discovered brain-wave frequency variations.

In my view, each of these individuals has completed one part of the billion-piece jigsaw puzzle, which forms the greater picture of a holistic understanding, of the human condition, consciousness and the Creator.

Let me conclude with a few questions we should think about:

1. How would you explain the world in 2018, if you went back in time to the year 1518? For example, how would you explain technologies such as the cell-phone or airplane? Would you not borrow jargon from an existing culture or field of science, such as "An object made from sand and metal that allows one to communicate with others around the world" or "A flying ship that allows one to travel great distances"? Despite the fact that an airplane looks nothing like a ship, would you not be forced to use language and terms relevant to the day? Likewise, if a visitor came from the year 2518, would he/she not be forced to use our current terminology to describe and explain his/her world? Perhaps the "Quantum Soul" is not related to quantum physics, but concepts remain true even if we lack the correct diction to describe them.
2. Are we really advancing forward as a human race? Perhaps we have merely found greater importance in different fields of study through various periods in history? Perhaps we have merely traded one skillset for another? Yes, we do have marvelous technology today, but do we have the survival skills of our ancient ancestors? Take Bear Grylls as an example; does he not have a vital skillset which has been lost in modern times?
3. Are hieroglyphics and cave art really primitive, or perhaps a more effective and efficient way to communicate? As the old saying goes: "A picture is worth a thousand words" would it not be more effective to communicate with pictures, and avoid possible language barriers?

4. If an archaeologist were to dig through your home 3000 years from now and find your latest gadget, would he/she not say, "I can't believe how backwards people were"? And yet you do not consider yourself backwards today. Whose perception of you is more correct, your own, or that of the archaeologist? Wouldn't you say that perceptions change with time?
5. Finally, if we are advancing forward, are we moving in the right direction? The ultimate question is, is the human race happier today than in other periods of history? Today we have both problems and solutions that did not exist a mere 100 years ago.

The second psychological bias or obstacle to overcome is:

Culture-centric - the tendency to view one's own culture as being superior. For numerous reasons both good and bad, people tend to think of their own culture as being the supreme culture. Unfortunately, this leads to conflict, and a mental block towards receiving new information which may challenge cultural belief systems. The Creator, however, is far beyond the limits of any single culture.

Ego-centric - the tendency to view one's self as being superior to others. For some individuals this is a mental disorder, such as narcissism or histrionic personality disorder. For others it is not a disorder but an inflated ego or arrogance. For others quite the opposite is true with feelings of worthlessness and a total lack of self-esteem. Whichever the condition, one thing remains true, namely a healthy self-esteem is required in the pursuit of greater knowledge. I hope to give you, the reader, a healthy sense of worth and purpose.

You need not apologise for your existence. Like wealth, feelings of self-worth are not evenly distributed among all the inhabitants of Earth - some have too much and some have too little.

As you will soon see, not every conversation is an argument, not every gathering is a competition, and one does not need to deflate another, to feel a sense of worth. The only failure one should fear, is not knowing what makes you different from others.

Some important questions to ask:

1. If I were born into an entirely different culture or religion, would I still hold the same views and opinions?
2. If I were born into a different race group, would I still hold the same views and opinions towards other races?
3. If I were born a different gender, would I still hold the same views and opinions towards the opposite gender?
4. If I were born in another period in history, would I still retain the views and opinions that I hold to be true today?
5. Am I fixated on ideas and beliefs which are harmful to others? Am I fixated in such a way that I am unable to develop?

There are, of course, many other psychological barriers, in terms of psychological biases.

One which is common, but less detrimental is that of the:

Bandwagon effect: - the tendency to do or believe things; because many other people do the same. (related herd behavior). This bias is often observed within individuals who lack a sense of self-identity.

I hope that through the lessons learned within, you as the reader, will be comfortable and knowledgeable, about who you are, and more importantly why you choose to belong or not to belong to a group.

Therefore, let us proceed with an open mind and critically challenge all preconceived ideas. In order for us to gain further insight and holistic knowledge into all that is, it is necessary to be aware of all cognitive biases and approach this subject with an untainted mind.

When one explores such subjects, it is important to keep in mind the two golden rules:

1. **To speak the truth is to be hated by all**. Very often, holistic statements are offensive to those who are sensitive about their race, culture or religion. However the path to wholeness requires "making a mess", as it were. As the old dictum goes, "What is right is not always popular, and what is popular is not always right." This work may offend readers, but I do so only for the greater good of holistic understanding. If you can tolerate subtle offences, and are curious to learn more, then read on. If you feel anger, hate or hostility within yourself when you confront a sensitive topic, then perhaps this book is not for you.

2. **Follow the money**. When one is at a loss to explain historical events, such as wars and conflicts, popular beliefs and misconceptions, politics and science, as well as many other topics, follow the money: look at who is profiting and by what means. This method often yields greater results than the most comprehensive research.

   This is not a conspiracy theory; although we will deal with conspiracy theories later on, this is by way of simple logical deduction. The logic is straightforward and without complexity; human beings require various inputs, to sustain their physical existence, such as food, water, shelter etc. These physical inputs are more often than not, cost-driven. Over a large span of history, man has had to pay for goods and services in order to sustain himself.

Human beings will often go to extraordinary lengths to make money. Of Sir Thomas More, Robert Whittington termed the phrase 'a man for all seasons'. Later, a poem of the same name by Robert Bolt compared the virtuous More with the phrase 'every man has his price', a theme which deals with the fallibility of the human being, to act in ways contrary to his essence, when faced with the prospect of receiving money.

Unfortunate but true; human beings will do some very strange and peculiar things to financially enrich themselves. This is driven by their need to sustain their physical existence, or in some occurrences, just pure greed.

We should bear this in mind when a logical progression suddenly stops or starts, for no apparent reason. Very often, money is the string which runs through all "the beads in the necklace", allowing us to connect seemingly unrelated events.

How man has complicated the issue:

Throughout the ages, the world has had individuals coming to Earth with a message. Whether we call these individuals, prophets, deities or any other title, the message has been the same - that a supreme being exists.

Whether we call this supreme being "Source", "Creator", "God" or any other name, is for the most part irrelevant.

Mankind has the tendency to view the world in terms of opposites, which we will discuss later on. However, the message is one.

To better grasp this concept, let us take a closer look at a common phenomenon:

Time zones:

- The Kiribati Islands are 12 hours ahead of Greenwich Mean Time (GMT +1200)
- The Midway Islands are 12 hours behind Greenwich Mean Time (GMT -12:00)

The distance between the Kiribati Islands and the Midway Islands is 806.2 Miles (1297.13 Kilometers), slightly more than the distance between Johannesburg and Cape Town in South Africa or London in the United Kingdom and Munich in Germany.

Despite the short distance between the Kiribati Islands and the Midway Islands, at:

- 9am on the 31st of December, 2017, in the Midway Islands, it is
- 9am on the 1st of January, 2018 on the Kiribati Islands.

It is the same Sun which is rising, but two entirely different dates for residents of each island. A man-made construction of time zones has made differences where there are none.

So too, if the "Message" is "The sun is rising", man will argue which day is about to begin, Sunday or Monday.

Unfortunately, mankind has an inherent need to be right; the messenger is discredited and the message is ignored. Thus, we have seen history repeating itself time and time again.

With the internet today, we have an abundance of information at our fingertips. However, information which is not indexed and categorized is for the most part useless. Perhaps one of the reasons Google has been so successful, is due to its indexing and categorizing of information, turning raw data into useful information.

Knowledge comes from useable information and not raw data; if we systematise and categorise what is already available, we can move forward with greater understanding.

Perhaps the reason humanity takes strides both forwards and backwards, is due to the time lag between acquiring new information and integrating the new with the old, finding harmony and consistency within the collective whole.

All too often, new thoughts and ideas are suppressed, as they violate conventional wisdom, only to become mainstream thought in the years to follow.

One such example is that of Ignaz Semmelweis, a medical doctor who discovered that hand disinfection could drastically reduce the spread of illness caused by unhygienic surgical practices.

Unfortunately for Semmelweis, his ideas were radical and broke conventional norms. His ideas lacked the scientific proof needed, due to the underdeveloped scientific principles of the time. This in turn, lead to Semmelweis's mental break-down and subsequent death, in a mental institution at the young age of 47.

Another such example is that of Nikola Tesla, who discovered that alternating current (AC) was more productive and useful than direct current (DC). He too was met with great skepticism, and died a poor and lonely man, only for later generations to accept that his ideas were in fact correct.

The human race can be absurdly stubborn, preferring to repeat the mistakes of the past, only to concede, to make the necessary changes when it is too late.

The Heater Analogy:

Imagine yourself on an icy cold winter's day - you are shivering, but in front of you is a fan heater. As you turn on the heater, you start to warm up. The shivering stops and before long, you are bonded with that heater; nothing can separate you from it. You have a natural desire to sit there and enjoy the warmth. The enjoyment is indescribable; you need not be coerced or forced, you are simply drawn to that heater and you want nothing to come in between you and your heat source.

Now imagine yourself on a sweltering summer's day. Every layer of clothing feels like a heavy blanket and you want nothing other than to cool down. In front of you is a fan heater; as you turn it on, you start to overheat and sweat starts dripping from every pore of your body. Sitting there is torture and you want to run a mile away.

The same fan heater, blowing hot air at the same temperature, has not changed, but depending on your circumstances, you are either drawn to it naturally or are naturally repelled.

The same can be said of spirituality; it is what it is. or more precisely, the Creator is, what it is, The Creator does not change, merely our perceptions and desire for closeness.

Depending on your circumstances, you are either naturally drawn towards it, without any coercion or societal pressure, and find yourself bonded to it in an inseparable way; or you are repelled.

When one is synchronised and balanced, the desire to be close to one's Creator does not involve any internal struggle, but rather a natural driving force. Just as the cold weather, naturally drives one close to the heater, so too is one naturally propelled towards the Creator.

This does not mean that no effort is required; rather the effort required seems to be trivial compared to the benefit of the warmth.

However, the same source of spirituality with all of its properties can also be repulsive. Coercion or societal pressure may keep you there in the short term, but at the first opportunity you will run a mile.

Spiritual enlightenment comes when the desire for greatness outweighs all other desires.

Throughout time, mankind has had a fascination with the origin of life. As living beings we know instinctively that we are capable of experiencing life in a profound way, with rich emotional experiences beyond the cold and sterile world of raw analysis. This work will seek to answer some of the basic questions related to the human condition, by stimulating curiosity and questioning all that we take for granted.

Asking the right questions will lead to more wisdom than having mediocre answers.

Asking the right questions will lead to more wisdom than having mediocre answers

Universal Laws of Existence:

No matter what culture, race or religion you belong to, we as human beings all share a common experience.

This experience is neither good nor bad. Sea water is just as salty for me as it is for you. Is the sea water bad because it is salty? On the one hand it sustains aquatic life, but on the other hand, drinking sea water can be fatal.

The laws of nature are absolutely neutral. A natural spring can provide you with life sustaining water, or it can drown you. The laws of nature are indifferent to your prejudices and biases.

For example, when either you or I stand in the rain, we both get just as wet, despite our different worldview and opinions. Rain water does not "care" about your beliefs or opinions.

My skin is burnt by fire to the same extent as yours; fire does not discriminate against race or religion. We are all bound by the laws of nature, like it or not. I may choose not to abide by a civil law, but I cannot choose not to abide by the law of gravity.

I was not consulted, nor did I vote in the law of gravity, and yet I am bound to abide. I may protest the law of gravity, but I am forced to adhere to it at all times. Even if I place myself within an anti-gravity chamber, I am still bound by its laws, because the moment I leave the chamber I resume experiencing gravity. I have not altered the law, but merely experienced weightlessness.

I may choose not to abide by a civil law, but I cannot choose not to abide by the law of gravity

Unbeknown to us, we are all bound to a set of laws which we did not create, nor consent to, and regardless, as citizens of planet Earth we all abide by the laws of nature. As we will soon see, just as there are laws which govern physicality, so too there are laws which govern spirituality. We as human beings are bound to these laws, whether we like it or not. The laws of the Creator govern our everyday lives, whether we know it or believe it, whether we like it or not.

Questions to ask:

1. Who made the laws of nature, and why?
2. By describing the process of how something works, have we addressed why it works? For example: why does the heart beat? Why do cells divide? Why does it rain? The question of "why" is not about the process; the process addresses the "how" question. If one was to tell you that it rains, because evaporation of water forms clouds etc. they are not answering the question, merely stating the process by which it happens.

With that out of the way, we are now ready to begin an exploration into the most profound subject matter that any entity can study.

3

THE AGE OF THE UNIVERSE

When we consider our planet, we are often misguided as to the size, age and capacity of planet Earth. Let us explore these concepts and once again raise some important questions.

How big is planet Earth?

Planet Earth has a circumference of approximately 40,000km. It has one natural satellite namely the Moon, which reflects light from the Sun, which is at the centre of our solar system. The circumference of the Sun is approximately 109 times greater than, that of planet Earth. Venus, which is usually the nearest planet to Earth, is approximately 40,000,000km away from planet Earth. To put this into perspective, if one were to travel in a commercial airliner traveling at a speed of 800km/h, it would take 50,000 hours or 2083 days of continuous travel to reach the destination.

Planet Earth is found within the Milky Way Galaxy, and is just a small speck within the galaxy. The Milky Way Galaxy is approximately 100,000 light years in diameter. To put this into perspective, if one were to travel at the speed of 1080,000,000 km/h for 100,000 years one would reach the edge of the Milky Way Galaxy.

In other words, if one traveled 1,350,000 Km/h (1.3 Million times faster than a commercial airliner), it would take 52,560,000,000 (52 billion hours) to reach the edge of the Milky Way Galaxy. There are an estimated 100,000,000,000 (100 Billion) observable galaxies within our known universe.

Considering the vast expanse of the known / observable universe, it is more than probable that there are several hundred thousand planets, like planet Earth, with a full range of bio-diversity. It would be rather closed-minded to assume that we as human beings are the only intelligent life form in the universe. We can safely assume that in this vast universe there are beings with far superior intellect compared to human beings. However this does not affect our purpose for being on planet Earth.

Universe or Multiverse?

The question of whether we have just one Universe, or Multiple Parallel Universes or even an infinite number of parallel universes is a matter of scientific debate. For purposes of our discussion, we can assume that there are in fact multiple Universes. Hence the probability of other life forms, including human-like life forms is very likely.

If this is in fact true, then the human race on planet Earth should consider themselves to be more similar than different, to all the other possible life forms which may exist. When one considers the bigger picture, it should become blatantly apparent, that the man-made constructs which separate us are almost negligible.

Despite our various ages, genders, socio-economic statuses, cultures, religions and races we all share a common bond, of being humans on planet Earth.

When one fully comprehends the magnitude and scale of our known / observable Universe, one can begin to appreciate the trivial differences that set us apart. Here once again, our culture-centric and ego-centric attitude precludes us from appreciating our similarities as human beings on a tiny planet called, Earth.

Some important questions to ask:

1. If the human race stands divided could we ever collaborate as a whole?
2. What would be the benefit of looking for similarities, rather than differences?
3. If there are so many places similar to planet Earth, then what are we doing here on this planet specifically?
4. Would you be bothered by mundane inconveniences if you were constantly aware of the bigger picture?
5. Is being aware of your tiny existence, negatively affecting your self-esteem?

The age of the Universe:

Many cultures and religions believe that planet Earth is a young planet, being in existence for only approximately 6000 years.

On the other hand, scientific methods postulate that Earth is substantially older, ranging from between 3.5 billion years old and 14 billion years old.

When one studies source texts, which will soon be quoted, we will see that both of these views are correct and accurate. Popular belief has tried for many years to place the scientific and religious beliefs as opposing views. However, nothing could be further from the truth. In fact today's science is complimentary to traditional views.

Even subjects such as evolution, which are often viewed as taboo within religious circles, can be sourced in texts dating back more than 1500 years ago.

Source text:

The vast majority of the texts sourced within this work will be Judaic in nature. Although by doing so, I will expose myself to culture-centric bias, I am aware of this fact.

I will thus take this into consideration, and make every effort to avoid a biased perspective, by illustrating which views are objective and which views are subjective.

From an objective stand point:

1. The Torah and its commentaries form the body of Judaic texts, which are ancient texts (dating back to more than 3000 years ago), and thus cover a broad range of subjects throughout many periods in history. Thus it serves as a great tool for exploration.
2. The authenticity and veracity of the Torah, as well as its lineage, have written and verifiable documented accounts, thus making it an authoritative text.
3. The Torah, with its commentaries and super-commentaries, comprise of at least 100,000 books, thus making it one of the most researched and documented ancient texts.
4. Many of the world's religions are based on the Old Testament a translation of the written Torah, thus serving as a basis for many individuals.

From a subjective stand point:

1. The Torah is the written word of the Creator, and thus carries significant weight within our discussions.
2. Every word of the Torah is absolutely true, even when it is difficult to comprehend.

3. My personal exploration into the existence of the Creator was learned directly from the Torah and its commentaries. Sharing my experience with the reader will entail using the very text which brought me to a greater understanding.

Returning to the age of the Universe, Rabbi Aryeh Kaplan, in his work[4], sources the opinion of the famous Sefer HaTemunah, attributed to Nehunya ben HaKanah, a 13th century Kabbalist, who is frequently quoted by Nachmanides and Rabbi Yosef Karo, who was the author of the last great codification of Jewish law in the year 1535, many centuries before modern day genetics and modern day science brought up the issue of the age of the universe.

According to the work of the Sefer HaTemunah, which cites the Talmud[5] that states that there were 974 generations before "Adam" was created. Furthermore he cites the concept that the world goes through 6000 years of creation, followed by 1000 years of rest, in accordance with the Sabbatical concept of six days of work and the seventh being a day of rest.

Moreover, just as we find the concept of a Jubilee (7 counting's of 7 years, totaling to a period of 49 years), so too within creation we find the concept of 7 countings of 7000 years, thus bringing the age of the Universe to 49,000 years. However, since space and time were elements of creation, these 49,000 years are not human years, but Godly years.

We know from several sources[6] that 1 Godly day is equal to 1000 human years. Thus, 1 human year which contains 365.25 days, and equates to 1 Godly year being 365,250 human years. Therefore, if our universe is 49,000 Godly years old, this will equate to 17,897,250,000 (close to 18 billion) human years old.

4 The Age of the Universe: A Torah True Perspective
5 Shabbos 88b
6 Psalms 90:4

As discussed extensively by the Tiferes Yisroel (Rabbi Israel Lifschitz (1782–1860)) in his commentary at the end of Seder Nezikin, what he called "Drush Ohr HaChaim", the story of Adam and Eve may have taken place during the latest cycle, occurring just close to 6000 years ago.

However, during the many other cycles of creation spanning 18 billion years, there were other creatures created which were similar to the modern day "Man".

As explained by the Tiferes Yisroel, the actual planet of Earth was created billions of years ago. However, the Creator refurbishes, or renovates the planet at the end of every cycle. The cycle begins with the creation of multiple species including; plant, animal and human life. This cycle completes its intended purpose and is then wiped clean of its contents, leaving just the bare rock of the planet exposed.

The cleaning process is done by using extreme weather conditions such as heat, cold, water etc., making it impossible for the various life forms to continue living. Planet Earth then lies fallow / desolate for 1000 Godly years, after which a new cycle is created with new species of plant, animal and human life, as well as new laws of nature.

This cycle has repeated itself several times, and thus it is not a contradiction but rather evidence that many fossilised species found today are no longer in existence.

Thus, if 7 cycles were to last a period of 18 billion years, each cycle would last approximately 2.57 billion years (There may even be sub-cycles within the cycle lasting for approximately 53,000 years, and sub-cycles within that lasting approximately 8000 years). Hence, a fossil dating back to 70,000 years ago is merely a creature dating back to two sub-cycles ago.

However, there is no evidence, that creatures of previous cycles evolved continuously in a linear fashion to what we have today. Each cycle and sub-cycle gave rise to its own set of unique species, as were required to fulfil the purpose of planet Earth during that particular time period.

Thus, dinosaurs were needed in their time period, but are no longer required today. Homo-Erectus had the functions needed to fulfil his task on planet Earth, but a new species was required for our current task.

What we do know, is that the purpose of the current cycle that we find ourselves in today, is an elevated purpose which includes mankind's unique role in perfecting him/herself, and for this reason the "Man" created in this particular cycle is quite different from the "Men" created in previous cycles.

An interesting side note: On Jewish marriage contracts, the date is always stated as "This day of this month of this year that we are counting" The emphasis is on the text which reads "This year that we are counting" as in order for the contract to be valid, the correct date must be used. We cannot accurately state the date without the caveat that this year is only "The year that we are counting" and not an absolute year.

Considering that we are living in a unique age where we now have the written words of the Creator, we are quite fortunate to be in existence for this ultimate goal which has taken so many years of development. Let us not squander this unique opportunity.

Another theory postulates that planet Earth is in fact a young planet dating back to a mere 6000 years.

According to this view, when the Creator created planet Earth he created a "Mature" planet, meaning that the Creator created rocks and fossilised material which would appear to be billions of years old.

Likewise, the Creator created mature animals, so that it was not a calf which was created, but a fully grown cow. Adam was not created as a young child, but as a fully matured adult.

According to this opinion, the Creator used what we might term an "illusion" to give off the appearance of an ancient world.

The reasoning behind this is that the Creator wanted to instill free choice into mankind. Thus, a window of opportunity to deny the Creator needed to be created, in order for mankind to search deeper, than the illusionary façade.

Thus, we may always, be confronted with alternate perspectives to allow for the truth to be discovered and not merely presented. One cannot claim to have discovered the truth unless the truth is somewhat hidden.

Some consider the latter argument to be intellectually fraudulent. However we cannot disprove this theory.

Questions to ask:

1. Does science complement or contradict religion?
2. Does the age of the Universe affect your daily routine?
3. Is where we came from, as important as, where we are going?
4. Are your responsibilities diminished if "Man" is an old creature?
5. If "Man" can evolve over time, can "Man" also worsen over time?

4

LIGHT ENERGY

A SOUL WITHIN A BODY

"What does it mean to be a human being?"

For centuries, philosophers, theologians, psychologists and even laymen have battled with the question: "What does it mean to be a human being?" We struggle to grasp a complete understanding of the human condition. We are so many things wrapped up into one; we have so many contradictions and yet we are driven to succeed.

Human beings are complex beings - we are more than just a body, and more than just a machine, or complex organism.

As human beings we are capable of thought, planning, memory, logic, creating, imagination and deep emotion. We build, we develop and we invent.

We see ourselves as sophisticated animals, despite the fact that we cannot communicate via sonar like the dolphin, bat or whale.

We think ourselves timeless despite the fact that unlike the lobster, we age.

We believe ourselves as capable, despite having a sense of smell, far worse than that of a mouse, bear or shark.

Our eyesight is many times worse, than that of the vulture, dragonfly or mantis shrimp.

Our hearing is profoundly worse, than that of a dog, bat or moth. Our physical strength ranks lowest amongst the apex predators. And so the list continues.

Despite all of this, "Man" believes that he is at the top of the food chain, the most intelligent of species and the best at conquering nature.

Maybe this belief is well-founded, or perhaps nothing could be further from the truth. With this open-ended question, let us explore further.

Questions to ask:

Using IQ (Intelligence Quota) as a referencing point:

1. If mankind's IQ falls within the range of 70-140, could there be other life forms in the universe, with relative IQ's between 700-1400, and 70,000-140,000? I.e., could there be life forms which are thousands of times more intelligent than us?
2. Is it not irresponsible for mankind, to eradicate entire species that we know nothing about?
3. Does the Universe as a whole, benefit from mankind's activities on planet Earth?
4. Considering mankind's arrogant and destructive nature, if mankind was to chance upon a creature with a relative IQ of 700, would humans simply want to eat it, instead of learning from it?
5. Considering the size of the Universe as previously discussed, as well as mankind's limited abilities and senses, is it not closed-minded to think that we are the most intelligent species in

the Universe? Could mankind be in the lower part of the overall intelligence spectrum?

Viktor Frankl on the human condition:

Viktor Frankl, a prominent psychologist and one of the founders of the branch of Psychology known as "Existential Psychology" strongly promoted the concept that the human being is more than a complex animal.

As human beings, we have properties not shared with the animal kingdom[7]
"Meaning is not something we create or invent. Meaning is found"

What makes the human being unique is not only the ability to think reason and speak, but something much more profound: the human being has a spirit, a soul which calls for meaning.

Frankl states in his work, Dimensional Ontology (1967), that there are three levels or dimensions of existence:

1. The Physical

2. The Psychological

3. The Spiritual

"If human behaviour is viewed from a sub-human (non-spiritual) level of being, the uniquely human or spiritual aspects of human existence will either be missed or seen in distortion."

[7] Personology – From the Individual to the ecosystem, WF Meyer et al, 2008 , Heinemann pp 436-462

To truly understand the human condition, one would need to understand:

1. Every last aspect of the human body, as well as all matters relating to the "physical". This would entail extensive collaboration with scientists from all fields of physical science, including doctors, mathematicians, physicists etc.)

2. Every last aspect of the human mind, as well as all matters relating to the "psychological" This would entail extensive collaboration with academics in the field of metaphysics, psychology and philosophy.

3. Every last aspect of the human spirit, as well as all matters relating to the "spiritual". This would entail extensive collaboration with all those who have profound knowledge of spirituality.

Finally, all three groups would need to collaborate, with each other, in order to create a complete body of understanding.

When we have this complete body of knowledge, we can then begin to understand the human condition.

Until such time, mankind will continue meandering in circles, debating whether or not a field of study even exists, and whether or not the arrogance of "Science A" is more than or less than the arrogance of "Science B". The futile work of non-collaboration has resulted in a burden on the back of the human race.

On the day that the complete body of knowledge is formed, it will be clear for all to see the Creator. Each person from each field of study will call the "Creator" by a different name, and relate to the "Creator" from their own perspective.

The scientific community may say we have found the "source energy" of all matter, the spiritualist will say we have found "**insert your deity here**". When in reality it was there all along hiding in plain sight.

The first hurdle to overcome is the realisation that human beings have unique qualities. It should be blatantly obvious, but as far as the search goes, many individuals get stuck at this point.

Science and philosophy - two inseparable quarks:

Sir Isaac Newton, a pioneer in the field of physical science was first and foremost a philosopher. This is not a coincidence; in order to prove a concept scientifically, one first needs to have an important question to ask, and then to seek answers to that question.

Philosophy can be viewed as the question, and science can be viewed as the answer. A question with no answer is incomplete, as is an answer with no question. As was stated previously, a good question, does more in terms of creating knowledge, than a mediocre answer does.

Just as two quarks can only be separated for a short period of time, so too by way of analogy, can physical science and philosophy remain separated as they have become in this current period of history.

Philosophy is born out of curiosity of the mind, as is physical science. The philosopher is aware that there is a need for "The Grand Unified Theory of Everything", and so is the scientist.

If science is not stimulated with questions, the answers remain pointless. Questions are the guiding force of science; philosophy has historically guided questions, which lead to scientific discovery.

In periods when human beings had the luxury of time to ponder questions, science moved forward. Conversely, in periods where human beings did not have the luxury of time to ponder deep questions, science stagnated. Similarly in periods when individuals were free to think of questions, science moved forward. However, in periods when individuals were suppressed from free thought and speech, science stagnated.

In this period, perhaps more than ever, a guiding force is needed to aim science in the right direction. We have an urgent need to know what to look for, and how to look for it. Repeating the same experiments of the past is by definition, stagnation. Peace on planet Earth is needed, even if for no other reason, than to allow mankind the opportunity to think, to question, and to find answers.

If not for the right set of circumstances, Sir Isaac Newton may never have seen the light of day. Had Albert Einstein not left Germany in 1933, we may have never known of his great insight.

Similarly, how many great, and world changing minds, have been pointlessly killed or stifled, due to mankind's, ape-like behaviour of war-mongering. Peace and collaboration are essential ingredients for long lasting, and sustainable development[8].

Questions such as "What causes planets to orbit?" or "How does light travel through a vacuum?" have motivated scientists to find answers.

Whenever science hits an "unknown" this is a clear indication that further questions are needed to solve the mystery. For example, it was widely believed that light needs a medium to travel through, until the discovery of electro-magnetism was made.

The mediocre answer given to the "light-question" at that time was: "There is in fact a medium through which light travels called the "aether", but we cannot observe it." The better answer involved the discovery of electro-magnetism.

Thus, it behooves us to ask philosophical questions pertaining to light and electro-magnetism, for herein lies the next frontier in the development of our greater understanding.

[8] As opposed to short growth spurts found at wartime.

Questions to ask:

1. If the Creator is called "light" can we discover the Creator by studying light?
2. Why does the speed of light remain constant?
3. Why it is that energy is inseparably related to light?
4. Why does the brain, and the heart (to a lesser degree) but not the kidney, operate using electro-magnetic energy?
5. Is having mass, limiting our ability to travel at the speed of light?
6. Is consciousness found within light?
7. Why does empty space contain energy?

Michael Newton - Journey of Souls:

The question of "What happens after we die?" has fascinated mankind for centuries. Michael Newton, Ph.D, is the founder of The Newton Institute for Life Between Lives Hypnotherapy In his books, he describes case studies using Past Life Regression hypnosis, as a means of therapy; and the details given by his clients, bear an uncanny resemblance to the spiritual science, as described by Rabbi Moshe Chaim Luzzatto in 1737.

If one needs empirical evidence that the human being lives on, after death, one can find a treasure trove within these case studies.

If not for the fact that the case studies parallel spiritual science, one may be tempted to view these case studies as mere suggestions offering no tangible truth. However, as we will discuss below, these case studies shed light on some fundamental principles of spiritual science.

In his books Journey of Souls: Case Studies of Life Between Lives (1994), as well as in Destiny of Souls: New Case Studies of Life Between Lives (2000), Newton describes the experiences and sensations felt by his clients, as they recall their previous life, and between life experiences.

Using Past Life Regression hypnosis, the author takes his client back in time to their "previous life" as well as their "life between lives". The fact that such a memory even exists, may be demonstrable proof that the essence of the human being is the Soul, which is not bound by a finite existence. Although many postulate that hypnosis may be nothing more than complex imagination at play, one will be hard-pressed to dismiss hypnosis entirely, as the human mind is a very complex structure.[9]

Common recurring themes:

1. The first recurring theme is that clients experience an "out-of-body" sensation when dying. Clients often report seeing their own body lying lifeless as they hover from "above" looking down.

2. Clients are initially in shock, having experienced consciousness while separated from their bodies.

3. Clients soon find their "true identity" as a spirit rather than as a human being.

4. Clients report having a "life review" in which they gain a full understanding of the life which has just ended.

5. Clients report, that their "true identity" is a light entity, which appears as various colours of the rainbow, ranging from yellow to violet depending on the "level of mastery" of the Soul.

[9] Igros Moshe Yoreh Deah Vol 3 Siman 44 (Hypnosis is permitted for medical purposes)

6. Clients report that they have been to planet Earth during various periods in history, and that in the "Soul World", planet Earth has a reputation for being one of the most difficult places for a soul to travel to.

7. Clients report that they have been sent to planet Earth to correct behaviors, usually related to self-control, I.e. they have been sent to planet Earth for a particular reason.

8. Clients report that there is a Creator, whom they all refer to as "Source"

9. Clients report that between lives, the Soul studies various ways of manipulating energy, with the ultimate goal of learning how to "create".

10. Clients report that when returning to a new human body, there is often difficulty readjusting to the restricted environment.

There are many more common themes of course. However for the purpose of this discussion we will focus just on the few items mentioned above.

Let us for a moment, postulate that all of the above is true and accurate, and let us ask why these items should hold true?

There may be many plausible reasons, why the themes reported by clients, are untrue, ranging from hearsay, to the very core understanding of how memory retrieval works, within the human brain.

Nonetheless, given our limited understanding of the human brain, and owing to the fact that neither the therapist nor the client had any reason to speak untruths, we can entertain that these reports are accurate.

Much like we do, when we take a news reporter's story at face value, and then dissect it using critical reasoning.

For example; when one hears a news report, regarding an "earthquake in Indonesia", we have no way of validating this information, without being present in Indonesia at the time of the alleged earthquake.

We thus rely, to a certain extent, on the eyes and ears of the news reporter, to give us an unbiased and truthful story.

In principle, a degree of trust exists between the news receiver and the news reporter. From the skeptical point of view, every news story is false until we have witnessed the event first-hand. Rightly so, any second-hand information is bound to be biased, and thus requires deep critical analysis.

In the same vein, if an event is reported to have occurred in the spiritual realm, we rely on the reporter to be our eyes and ears in the said location.

The reporter in this case is the client, and thus we can treat information obtained as a "news report".

It is for this reason that corroborating of evidence is required before validating this information. When we contrast the work of Luzzatto, Penrose and Hameroff with that of Newton, many consistencies are found, thus indicating that certain principles and truths have emerged from entirely different perspectives and fields of science, which corroborate one another.

Unraveling the recurring themes:

a) As with many reported out-of-body experiences, people often view their bodies from "above". This would be understandable, since while a person is in a body, their consciousness or spirit is held down by the physical body, due to the force of gravity.

Thus the spirit or consciousness is constantly counteracting gravity in an effort to remain attached to the physical body. Much like a helium balloon, which is weighted down, when the weight is removed from the balloon, the balloon moves upward naturally.

The same holds true for consciousness or spirit; when the weight of the body is removed, its natural flow will move it in an upward direction. This may explain why so many individuals report "looking down" since their free consciousness has moved upward relative to their environment.

b) We know that when light is separated through a prism, it divides into its elemental colours, namely: red, orange, yellow, green, blue, indigo and violet. The Prophet Ezekiel[10] described his journey into the spiritual realm, with the sight of spirits ranging in colour, as well as spirits which appeared as pure white light:

"Like the appearance of a rainbow which is seen in the clouds, on a rainy day"

This could explain the phenomenon, of white light separating into its various colours, and that the spirit is best described in terms of light energy.

c) The "Sefer Yetzirah" - The Book of Creation[11], gives a detailed account of the mechanics behind creation. I have used this work, together with the works of Rabbi Moshe Chaim Luzzatto to create a "map" of the spiritual realm. I will discuss this "map" in detail below.

[10] Ezekiel 1:15 and 1:28

[11] Originally authored in the 6th century and translated by Rabbi Aryeh Kaplan

Some of the concepts which are discussed in the Book of Creation, are found within many works of the early Kabbalists. For the purposes of our discussion there are several concepts which one needs to understand, to appreciate the texts.

1. The soul is made up of several parts, (In ranking order from lowest to highest), namely:

    - "Nefesh" (Life Force)
    - "Ru'ach" (Spirit)
    - "Neshama" (Soul)
    - "Chaya" (Living Energy)
    - "Yechida" (Uniqueness)

The translations are not accurate, but for our purpose, all we need to know is that the soul, like the human body is made up of multiple codependent systems.

2. There are four dimensions to reality, (In ranking order from lowest to highest), namely:

    - "Olam Ha Asia" (The world of doing) - Energy in this dimension is manipulated through physical actions.
    - "Olam Ha Ye Tzira" (The world of formation) - Energy in this dimension is formed in preparation for the "Olam Ha Asia" (The world of doing).
    - "Olam Ha Bri-yah" (The world of creation) - Energy in this dimension is created from non-existence in preparation for the "Olam Ha Ye Tzira" (The world of formation)

- "Olam Atzilus" (The world of intimacy) - "Energy" in this dimension is prepared for non-existence.

Creation is a wave of energy - varying the frequency produces various forms of creations:

3. The beings responsible for each level are unique and function according to their intended purpose. For the purpose of our discussion namely that of creation, we will discuss the "Ofanim" (spinning energy), in greater detail. Creation/Formation, or the process of going from existence to formation is done using a process of "spinning energy".

Creation/Formation requires "rotation" or a "stopping and starting" or "on and off" motion. The best analogy is found in the human body, with the heart pumping or lungs breathing or synapsis in the brain firing.

In order for these systems to function, they require a cyclic motion, such as "breathing in" and "breathing out", or "pumping in" and "pumping out". Another analogy can be found in the "binary" system of digital electronics; a system of "on" and "off" positions are used to transmit information, or turn "nothingness" into "something-ness". Said another way, to turn "meaninglessness" into "coherent-ness".

When energy is cycled in such a fashion; a frequency or wave is produced, i.e. the interval between two "pumps in" or two "on activities".

As we know light energy of different frequencies or wave lengths produces various colours. Hence all creation is centred on the creation of frequencies or wave-like motions, sometimes referred to as vibrations.

When the frequency is too high or too low, our ability to perceive with our senses is lost. Frequencies which fall outside of our perceptual abilities are called spiritual, as we will discuss shortly.

4. "Hish-tal-shelus" (energy flow) - For the purpose of our discussion it is important to be aware of the concept of "energy flow". Like running water, which naturally flows from an elevated point to a sunken point, so too does energy flow from a high point to a low point. In order for energy to be preserved, it must pass through a series of transformations.

This concept is best understood using the analogy of Alternating Current (AC). As discovered by Nikola Tesla, by increasing and decreasing the voltage using a transformer to step up or step down the voltage, electricity can be transmitted over great distances while preserving the energy.

The 10 "Sefiros" (which has no direct translation or meaningful term) is a concept in spirituality, whereby high forms of energy can be transmitted across various dimensions by stepping down the energy using spiritual transformers.

Another way of viewing the 10 Sefiros is by way of comparison to the common telephone. The input of the sound produced by the talker is converted into an electric current, which is then sent across the phone lines, and then decoded from electric current back into audible sound, on the receiving end. In this way we can view the 10 Sefiros as a communication device.

Perhaps another good analogy, which can help us understand the 10 Sefiros, is by way of how information is transmitted via the Internet. When one sends an e-mail for instance, the information is transmitted in packages of data, which are transformed several times, as the data is routed to its final destination, and finally back into legible text and pictures on the recipient's end.

Rabbi Moshe Chaim Luzzatto (1707 - 1746)

The following are quotes taken from Rabbi Moshe Chaim Luzzatto:[12]

The way of God: (Part 1 Fundamentals / 5. The spiritual realm):

- "The spiritual consists of all entities which are not physical and which cannot be detected by physical means."
- "[The spiritual entities] are also divided into two categories souls and transcendental beings."
- "Souls comprise a class of spiritual entities created to be put into physical bodies."
- "Transcendental beings comprise a class of spiritual entities that are not created to be put into physical bodies"
- "[Transcendental beings] are also divided into two categories. The first category consists of forces (Kochos), and the second, of Angels."
- "These transcendental beings also exist on different levels, each type having its own laws and distinct nature."
- "There… is another class that is like an intermediate between the spiritual and the physical…namely that of Shedim."
- "Of all things that exist, however, only man alone consists of two absolute opposites, namely a spiritual soul and a physical body. Nothing else in all creation shares this quality"

[12] Derech Hashem – The way of God, Translated by Rabbi Aryeh Kaplan: 1977, Feldheim, New York, USA

Mesilas Yesharim – The path of the Just, Translated by Yosef Leiber:2004, Feldheim, New York, USA

- "One of these fundamentals is that everything in the physical world has a counterpart among the transcendental Forces."
- "Every physical entity and process is under the charge of some type of angel"

The way of God: (Part 2 Providence / 5. How Providence Works)

- "The Creator arranged all created things in a system of steps and sequences"
- "The Creator thus first influences an angel, who in turn influences another angel on a lower level. This continues step by step until the final angel acts upon a physical thing."
- "The Creator showed and informed the Roots of all created things of their true essence and nature, as well as the purpose for which they were created."

The way of God: (Part 2 Providence / 6. The system of providence)

- "In the heavenly courts of justice, all the truly relevant considerations for any matter are brought forward and revealed."

The way of God: (Part 2 Providence / 8. Details of providence)

- "In this respect, the history of mankind is very much like the life of an individual, for as an individual is born and grows to maturity, so too, the human race."

The way of God: (Part 3 The Soul, Inspiration, and Prophecy / 1. The soul and its influence)

- "This higher Soul is placed in man only in order to give him a connection to the spiritual roots."
- "The Divine Soul is joined to the animal soul, which in turn is joined to the most ethereal element of the blood."
- "As a result of this connection, whereby the Divine Soul is linked to the body…the Devine Soul becomes limited in certain respects."
- "Even though this Divine Soul is often referred to as a single entity, it actually consists of a number of parts."
- "The Creator also designed that the bond between the body and the Divine Soul should be somewhat loosened while a man sleeps. The portion of the Soul - Ruach (Spirit) and above then rise and sever themselves from the body. Only the portion Nefesh (Life Force) remains with the lower soul. The freed portions of the Soul can then move about in the spiritual realm wherever they are allowed."

The Path of the Just: (Introduction and Chapter 1 Man's duty in his world)

- "Piety, therefore, is construed by people to consist of the reciting of many Psalms, making very long confessions, undertaking difficult fasts and performing ablutions in ice and snow, all of which are incompatible with intellect and reason."
- "Is it befitting our intelligence that we exert ourselves and labor in speculations concerning that which we have no obligation, in

fruitless debates and empty Pilpul[13]....while the great obligation that we owe our Creator we abandon to habit and rote?"

- "In summation: a person was not created for his position in this world."
- "Therefore, you will surely understand that no intelligent person could believe that the purpose of man's creation relates to his position in this world."

[13] Intellectual Torah discussions, void of emotional integration. – Also known as "Mental Gymnastics" and "Soul Suppression"

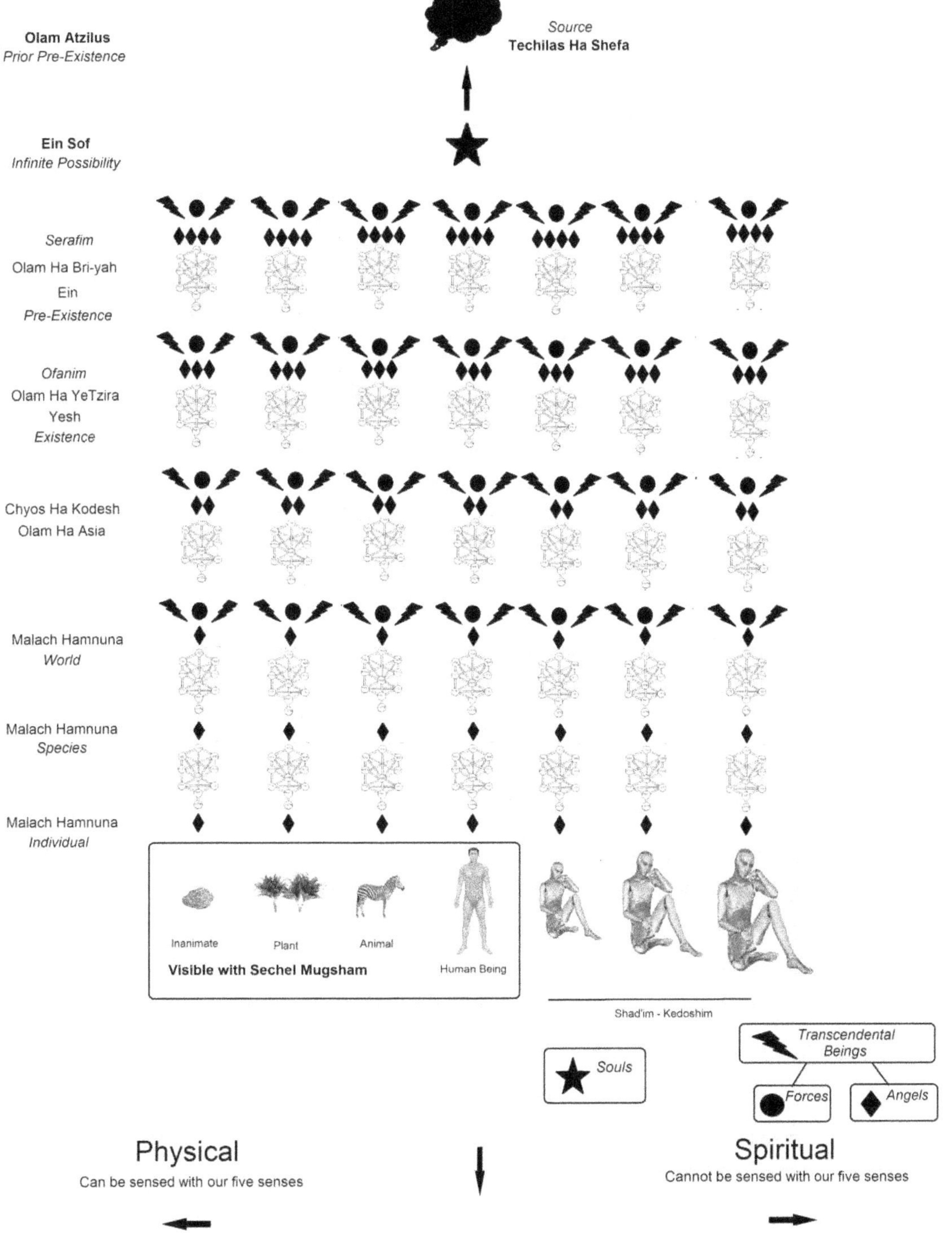

Physical

Can be sensed with our five senses

Spiritual

Cannot be sensed with our five senses

The Spiritual Map explained:

1. In the centre we have a divide between the physical and the spiritual. As explained above, the physical consists of all items which can be sensed with our five senses. The spiritual consists of all that, which cannot be sensed with our five senses.

2. As we move along the bottom row from left to right, we find a spectrum of created beings which increase in spirituality, or dynamic life.

   - To the extreme left, we find "the inanimate" objects which are purely physical.
   - Moving over, we find "plant" life, which is more "alive" than the inanimate.
   - Next we find, "animal" life which in turn is a level of existence higher than that of plant life.
   - Next we find "Human Being" life, which in turn is a level of existence higher than that of animal life.
   - Moving along, we find "Shad'im" life, which in turn is a level of existence higher than that of human being life. Although Shad'im are depicted as humanoid like creatures, they have the ability to transform into any physical shape.
   - The "Leviyoson" or Leviathan falls into this category of hybrids between physical and spiritual, consisting mainly of a spiritual component and only a small portion being

physical. Its natural physical shape is likened to that of a whale[14].

- The difference in potential between "Plant" life and "Inanimate" life is as great as the difference between any other species along the spectrum. There is no comparison between the level of complexity and intellect found in a rock, to that found in a plant. Similarly, an animal is far more complex and intelligent than a plant.

[14] See Ben Yo hadah – Avoda - Zara 4a

3. Above each species is an Angel, which is responsible for the maintenance of that particular species.

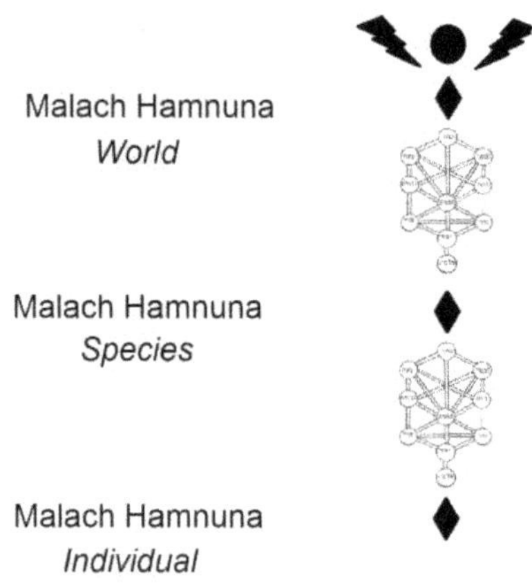

4. This Angel in turn receives its energy from a superior Angel above it. Its energy is received via the "Sefiros", as we mentioned above.

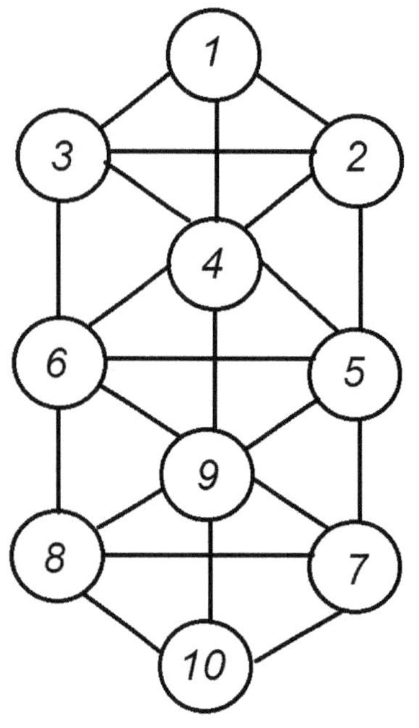

The names of the various channels through which energy passes through, as well as their function and order, is a topic of discussion in its own right.

As you will notice, there is no direct path between energy channels 6 to 7.

The centre channels are used to contain and transmit energy flows. Channel 9 therefore has to receive energy from channels 5, 6, 7 and 8 and then deliver all the energy into channel 10.

Channel 9 is therefore the most potent channel, while Channel 10 is merely a receptacle.

Channel 1 is the highest form of energy, while channel 10 is the lowest.

5. Each level receives its energy source, from the level above it. Hence, on the highest plane, non-existence or pre-existence is transformed into existence. The next level down then takes that existing energy and forms it into a more meaningful existence - this is termed "formation". The next level down then utilises this energy and transmits it to the first level, which ultimately acts upon a physical being.

6. As you will notice, the Soul comes from an incredibly high level, the world of infinity. This world is above all the other forces and entities. It is specifically because of this fact, that the human being which comprises of both a body and Soul, is truly unique from other species. The fact that the Soul is so tremendously

powerful, enables the human being to be connected to the Source in an intimate way.

7. The Source or Creator is not found within the spiritual system, but acts upon it from above, to facilitate the continuous existence of all that exists.

Technically speaking, if one were to say that the Creator doesn't exist, one would be correct, since the Creator occupies the realm of "prior pre-existence".

In human terms, this realm does not exist; existence in human terms only begins in the realm of "Olam Ha YeTzira" the realm of "Yesh" or existence.

The Creator is deliberately "hidden" in a realm of "prior pre-existence", since the "energy" level of the Creator would "overload" the system. The Creator had to deliberately "step-down" the "energy" to allow ambiguity, imperfection and choice to exist in the physical world. Hence, we find the need for so many layers of separation.

The Creator is there, however, but does not conform to our understanding of existence. Likewise, the Soul is there, originating from the realm of "infinite possibility" inside the human being, but also, does not conform to our understanding of existence.

The only way to detect things which are there, but do not exist is to compare two states of being, one with the said presence, and one with the said presence removed.

For example, a human being with a Soul is alive, while a human being with the Soul removed is dead. The most simple of people can differentiate between a living and a dead human being. The presence of the Soul represents all that is different, between a living human being and a dead human being. Those who are wise will understand.

8. You will also notice that only a very small portion of reality is visible in our state of "Awake Consciousness"[15]. We will deal with this concept in further detail later on.

On closer examination, many of the common recurring themes described by Newton's clients resemble the works of the early Kabbalists whose writings pre-date the client's sessions by many centuries.

Albeit that the two fields merely complement each other in many regards, one cannot state categorically that the reports made by the clients are false.

Thus, barring any evidence to the contrary we may tentatively accept the "news report" as being true and reliable in nature.

Stuart Hameroff and Roger Penrose

Dr. Stuart Hameroff is a Professor of Anesthesiology and Psychology. Sir Roger Penrose is a mathematical physicist, mathematician and philosopher of science.

[15] There are 32 different types of consciousness – See Appendix II – In Sefer Yetzira pp 297

Dr. Hameroff and Sir Penrose, postulated a theory of consciousness[16] known as the Orch OR theory. Orch OR suggests that there is a connection between the brain's bio-molecular processes and the basic structure of the universe.

Many of the concepts found within this theory, also give credence to traditional Kabbalistic views, as well as many Eastern philosophies regarding the nature of the human body and Soul.

- Hameroff maintains that consciousness can remain intact post-partum, via quantum entanglement.

- Furthermore, Hameroff maintains that consciousness resonates within the microtubules found within the neurons of the brain, as a result of vibrations.

- Consciousness is usually found when electroencephalogram (EEG) readings measure a beat frequency of 40 Hertz.

One interesting discovery made, using the EEG, found that there is a sudden spike in brain activity just after death, comparable to that of wakefulness.

Another interesting observation was made in some patients who had suffered from cardiac arrest, and had been pronounced clinically dead.

These patients reported having a "near-death-experience" (NDE), in which their consciousness left their bodies, and they were able to view their bodies from above. These patients were subsequently revived, and had a full recollection of the events which had transpired.

[16] Consciousness in the universe A review of the 'Orch OR' theory, 2013, Elsevier, Physics of Life Review, pp 39-78

Penrose and Hameroff concluded that consciousness plays an intrinsic role in the Universe, and it is through what is termed the "Quantum Soul" that we experience reality.

These NDEs described by cardiac arrest patients also bear a resemblance, to the actual death experience, as described by Newton's clients mentioned above.

The theme of one being able to view one's own body from outside of one's body, seems to be a reoccurring theme found across multiple disciplines and fields of study. This would seem to indicate that a fundamental principle is at play, a principle that has not yet been fully understood by modern-day science.

The human Condition:

In conclusion, based on the research of multiple scholars, from multiple disciplines, and multiple fields of study, and across multiple periods of history, one can make the reasonable assertion that the human being, can best be described as a: a physical body with a spiritual soul, or a spiritual soul with a physical body.

Whether we call the Soul a "spark of God" or a "Quantum Soul" or "Atma" or "Atman" or any other name, it is just a matter of semantics.

Regardless of our point of departure, we reach the final conclusion; namely the essence of the human being is far more than a material body.

Questions to ask:

1. Is our material mindset hindering or enhancing, our life satisfaction?
2. Why do all known particles contain a spinning energy?
3. Why is there so much "empty" space in atoms?
4. Is there a reason why planets need to orbit?

5

MEANING AND INNER PEACE

Three types of human beings that can tolerate planet Earth:

Whichever way you reach the conclusion, that the human being has a spirit, be it through science, spirituality, religion, culture, reason, emotion, awareness or a personal life experience, you may find yourself searching for meaning and a greater understanding.

Questions to ask:

1. Why do I have a Spirit/ Soul?

2. Is there a purpose to my existence?

When we examine the nature of the Soul as described in the spiritual "map", a few noteworthy points can be observed.

1. The Soul emanates from a spiritual domain, exceeding that of the most advanced and powerful Angels. Hence as human beings, we have the potential to be superior to Angels.

2. The Soul emanates from the domain of prior-pre-existence; hence the human being is exceptionally complex in all manner of ways.

3. The Soul emanates from a domain intimately associated with the Creator. Hence every human being has an automatic intimate

connection to the Creator of all. There is no need for any intermediary, since we are already connected at the highest possible level.

4. The human being is truly unique, comprising of two opposite factors, namely a physical body and a spiritual Soul. The alert human being is always in constant turmoil, torn between two entirely opposing forces.

5. Owing to the loftiness of the Soul, no physical cure or remedy can bring satisfaction or relief to a troubled Soul. Hence, the pain experienced by a troubled Soul is a pain so deep that it defies human comprehension.

6. If you were fully aware of the capacity and potential of the Soul, you would in all likelihood worship yourself as a God. Individuals who have achieved great success often become entirely egotistical, as this is a logical progression. It is for this reason that the human race often gets caught up in the worship of "Man". We will come back to this point a little later.

7. When we acknowledge the existence of the Soul, we develop the utmost reverence for humanity. However, when we deny the existence of the Soul and the Creator, we rob ourselves of a rich and meaningful life, and we cheapen human existence.

8. Owing to the loftiness of the Soul, and its tremendous power, the human race is in a position to achieve unbelievable greatness. As I discussed in my previous work "Fundamentals of Judaism" greatness does not equal goodness. One can be exceptionally great, but one can abuse the power of greatness to commit atrocities. The ultimate state of the human being is Greatness combined with goodness.

9. Every human being is worthy of having an autobiography made and studied. Of the approximately 107 billion human beings that have lived on our planet throughout history, the life story of most individuals remains untold: "History is always written by the winners."[17] However, the story of the losers is equally as important.

For a great many human beings, planet Earth is quite intolerable; research shows that the attainment of wisdom brings increased distress (Staudinger and Gluck, 2011)[18] . As King Solomon said, "For in much wisdom is much aggravation, and he who increases knowledge, increases pain"[19].

When one comes to the realization that the Soul is a free spirit unbridled with concepts of space and time, and unhindered by physical constraints, emotionally free from any burden and immortal in its existence, one will begin to realise that although the physical body is a useful tool to enable dynamic interaction in a physical world, for the most part the Soul is in essence a prisoner within the human body, barely capable of attaining even the slightest pleasure. The Talmud[20] tells us that the Soul is able to see from one side of the world to the other, until it enters the human body. Thus, the Soul is extremely unsatisfied with its physical entrapment. The pleasure experienced by a happy Soul is unearthly; likewise the pain felt by a troubled Soul is so deep and immense, so that physical compensation does little to alleviate the pain. The Soul is accustomed to immediate gratification of immense magnitude. We will come back to this point when dealing with Human Development.

[17] Dan Brown - The Da Vinci Code (2003) Doubleday (US) Transworld & Bantam Books (UK)

[18] Adult Development and Aging, Cavanaugh and Blanchard-Fields 7th ed (2015), Cengage, Stamford, US, pp 212

[19] Ecclesiastes 1:18

[20] Niddah 30b

There are only three types of human beings which can tolerate planet Earth:

1. The Super-Rich
2. The Super-Patient
3. The Super-Stupid

There are only three types of human beings which can tolerate planet Earth:
The Super-Rich
The Super-Patient
The Super-Stupid

The Super Rich:

Individuals who are trillionaires many times over, and can afford to meet every demand, desire and need spontaneously without any concern for the cost involved, may find that planet Earth is tolerable, or even a pleasant environment.

This group of people has the freedom to do almost anything that they want, exactly when they want to. The fulfilment of their desire does not incur any waiting whatsoever, and thus their Spirit experiences a degree of freedom whilst contained within a human body.

This group of individuals does not include poorer individuals who are concerned with growing, protecting and managing their wealth. These activities disturb the spirit with worry.

In order for wealth to satisfy the spirit, it has to be abundant enough to replenish itself continuously without intervention. In addition, the desire must relate to that which is material.

The Super-Patient:

The next group of individuals has a unique ability to endure and wait patiently for their desires to be met. If you are the kind of person who can wait until you are 45 years old, to get the tricycle you wanted when you were 3 years old, then you are probably a part of this group.

The level of patience required for this category of individuals is saintly and noble. In essence these individuals have no tangible desires, and are therefore not frustrated by the time differential, between desire and gratification of desire. For such individuals their spirit is free since they possess an abundance of patience.

Included in this group are Buddhist monks, Angel-like human beings and those who have absolute control over their every wish and desire. The Super-Patient can tolerate every inconvenience and trouble, and are thus able to tolerate planet Earth with its many frustrations.

The Super-Stupid:

For this group of individuals, nothing more is needed in life, than a bag of pretzels and a can of beer. These are the dimwitted individuals with an extraordinary level of stupidity. Individuals such as these, make Darwin's theory of evolution seem plausible. As the dictum goes, "Ignorance is bliss". This group of individuals has the unique advantage of ignorance, much like an ape in the jungle, which is fearless, when jumping across trees at a great height.

The ape can enjoy the freedom of movement, while human beings, with a developed prefrontal cortex, weigh out the risks of jumping from great heights, and therefore elect not to jump across the trees. Thus, human beings have far less pleasure from trees than apes do, due to their increased intelligence. The ape however is not burdened by fear, and thus views the jungle as an immense playground. The human being, in contrast, views the jungle as a place packed with danger.

Similarly, the "Super-Stupid" see planet Earth as an immense playground, and are completely oblivious to the dangers which surround them[21]. One can almost be envious of such individuals, for their uncalculated risks often come with financial gains. Much like the ape who climbs a tree perched upon a cliff, and finds food to sustain itself, without the realisation of the danger involved, this group of individuals succeeds in almost every endeavor. As the verse says, "The Creator protects the fool."[22]

Which one are you?

The next time you feel the sensation, "Isn't life just great?", check your bank balance perhaps you have become a multi-trillionaire. If not, check your back, perhaps you have grown "Angelic Wings", if that is also not the case, well then, what is there left to say…

For many individuals who don't snugly fit, within one of the three aforementioned categories, planet Earth is a difficult and challenging environment for the body, mind and soul.

A human being with a Spirit has no real place on planet Earth. The drudgery of existence, and having to continuously maintain this state of existence, can be the most unpleasant of all experiences. One may even feel that abortion is the greatest gift that one can give to a child. To not exist in a human body on planet Earth may be a far sweeter deal.

If you are an individual who has come to this realszation, then you are heading in the right direction. You are perfectly normal and sane, because to live is to constantly be challenged. There is no shame in suffering; you are merely becoming a greater person. You are in search of the Creator.

[21] Shabbos 13b

[22] Psalms 116: 6

An intelligent creature with unbridled selfishness:

To begin to understand the "Human Condition", let us look at a fairly well-known story, with a lesser known consequence:

The story is related to us in the book of Genesis[23] regarding a city named Sodom. We are told that this city is inherently corrupt, and is eventually destroyed. This story is well-known for the most part.

What is not as well-known, is the extent to which the city of Sodom was corrupt. The Talmud[24] and Midrash[25] explain that the city of Sodom was a physically beautiful city, which was well maintained, and prosperous in every aspect.

The residents of the city of Sodom were upper-class people, the elite of society; well-mannered, cultured individuals which were law-abiding at all times.

Sodom was the closest thing to Utopia as could be, and its residents were adamant that it remain that way.

In order to maintain this picture-perfect city, Sodom had by-laws restricting travel into the city and had exceptionally high taxes, to discourage the less fortunate from settling there. Sodom was the city of choice for the rich and famous.

We are told of a story of a beggar, who visited Sodom hoping to find a generous handout from any one of the many wealthy individuals.

To the beggar's surprise, at every door that he knocked on, he was greeted, in a warm and friendly manner by the home owner who promptly gave him a coin.

---

[23] Chapters 13-18

[24] Sanhedrin 109a

[25] Bereishis Rabah 48

The beggar, who had not eaten in days, took his collected charity and proceeded to the market-place to purchase some food.

The first food store that he entered refused to take his coins; he then proceeded to the next food store where his coin was again refused. As he continued, not a single store in the market-place allowed him to purchase food.

Dehydrated and starving the beggar, crawled towards the entrance of the market place, where he died.

The townspeople then rushed in and retrieved their coins, which they had carefully marked with their names, from the dead beggar.

The rotten attitude in Sodom was clear-cut:

"It's my money, go and earn your own" and
"Your problem isn't mine"

Of course, slamming the door in the beggar's face would be uncultured and impolite, so the people acted with a facade of "hospitality".

When we view this story in Genesis with its commentaries, it becomes clear that the city of Sodom could be like any modern-day city today, and its inhabitants just as corrupt as any modern-day society.

The human being, can be the most vile and selfish creature, void of all human emotions and empathy. The human being reaches its low point when aesthetics comes before human dignity.

Sodom represented all that is vulgar in the human race, a perfunctory courtesy masking an agenda of complete apathy towards others.

Finding pleasure in the suffering of others:

Throughout time, mankind has found numerous ways of deriving pleasure from watching and participating in the suffering of others.

Today, overtly psychopathic behaviour is frowned upon by society at large. However, the root cause and desire are still present, thinly veiled and ever-present as part of the human condition.

In ancient Greece, great festivals[26] were celebrated with the explicit purpose of watching human beings being tortured to death for pure entertainment value[27].

One ancient pagan ritual which is particularly revealing, is the service of a pagan God named Molech. This service entailed, creating two big bonfires with a space between. Parents among the worshippers would then hand over their child to the priests of Molech, who would stand at adjacent sides of the two bonfires, and pass the child through the flames, back and forth until the child was burnt to death[28].

The human being is capable of all forms of depravity and cruelty. The human being is also capable of the greatest acts of love, kindness and compassion. What kind of human being you wish to become, is up to you.

The Development of the Human Character:

As human beings, we grow and develop, from an embryo to a fetus, from a fetus to an infant, from an infant to a child, and so on. Whereas the growth and development which takes place externally, can easily be monitored, and is apparent to all, the internal growth however, namely

[26] Talmud Avoda Zara 11b and 18b – Rashi ibid

[27] http://en.wikipedia.org/wiki/Brazen_bull

[28] Vayikra – Leviticus 18:21 – Rashi ibid

the growth and development of the mind, and its abilities, are far harder to detect and monitor.

Moreover, the internal growth and development, i.e. growth of the mind, has several unrelated components such as, memory, intelligence, cognition, emotion, and so on, all of which follow their own separate path, of growth and development.

When we speak of the development of the human character in this context, we will be speaking of the emotional development, and more specifically the emotional and moral development of the human mind, namely how do we, build and develop a working emotional framework, with which we view the world around us. We will address intellectual and cognitive development separately, in a later part of this book.

As we stated above, it is easy to monitor our external growth. For example, if an adult has not grown taller since the age of infancy, the problem is blatantly obvious. However, when an adult has the moral development of an infant, the problem may go completely undetected for many years.

Determining whether or not an individual is selfish or selfless, is dependent on whether or not an individual has reached emotional and moral maturity; selfish individuals can be said to be emotionally and morally immature, whereas selfless individuals can be thought of as having reached emotional and moral maturity.

Since intellectual and emotional/moral development, each take a separate path of growth, it is perfectly possible, and in fact quite common, to see individuals who are functioning as adults in the cognitive domain, but as pre-school children in the emotional domain.

In a world which is geared wholeheartedly towards material consumption, emotional and moral development can go completely unchecked for years.

When we examine the natural path of emotional and moral development, it will become clear to see, that many individuals in positions of power, are in fact pre-school children when it comes to emotional and moral choices. This has a catastrophic effect on the subjects of such individuals.

The debate as to whether or not our personality evolves during adulthood is a matter of contention between scholars. Jean Piaget and Carl Jung[29] were amongst the first to theorise the notion of personality development. Erik Erikson also theorized about the development of personality throughout the lifespan, and went a step further to state that this development occurs in a sequential order. Loevinger[30], based on Erikson and Sullivan[31], created a model which describes the sequences of personality development throughout the lifespan.

However, theorists such as Costa and McCrae[32] maintain, that personality traits develop only up until the age of 30, after which they remain fairly stable.

What is not a matter of contention though, is that individuals develop their personality during infancy, childhood and adolescence, and further development, is not achieved by all.

[29] Adult Development and Aging, Cavanaugh and Blanchard-Fields 7th ed (2015), Cengage, Stamford, US, pp 253-254.

[30] Ego Development, Loevinger, J. (1976), San Francisco, Jossey-Bass

[31] Interpersonal Theory and Psychotherapy, Developmental Epochs of childhood through adolescence, (1946)

[32] Adult Development and Aging, Cavanaugh and Blanchard-Fields 7th ed (2015), Cengage, Stamford

Based on Loevinger's model, I will try to demonstrate the unique relationship which exists between the mind and the Soul. I have termed this relationship **"Soul-Chology ©"** which is a contraction of words, combining the field of study relating to the Soul with the field of study relating to the mind[33].

Stages of Development: (Erikson[34])

Approximate Age	Character Trait	Psychosocial crisis
0-2 years	Hope	Basic trust vs. mistrust
2–4 years	Will	Autonomy vs. shame and doubt
4–5 years	Purpose	Initiative vs. guilt
5–12 years	Competence	Industry vs. inferiority
13–19 years	Fidelity	Identity vs. role confusion
20–39 years	Love	Intimacy vs. isolation
40–64 years	Care	Generativity vs. stagnation
65-death	Wisdom	Ego integrity vs. despair

Erikson believed that as we grow older, we are faced with different "crises"; successful resolution of the crises creates a character trait within the individual. In the early years, an individual learns to trust and mistrust, and if learnt correctly, the trait of "Hope" will develop within the individual.

33 The topic of "Soul-Chology ©" will be dealt with in a separate work dealing exclusively with this subject.

34 Identity and the Life Cycle, Erikson, (1980), New York, Norton and Company (See Wikipedia)

One who is unable to trust will be unable to feel a sense of hope. As the individual grows, the next challenge is learning when and how to act with the environment, when this is achieved successfully, the trait of "Will" emerges within the individual.

One who does not know how and when to act with the environment, will face problems of lethargy. The next challenge is taking responsibility for one's actions, and if completed successfully, will lead to the trait of "Purpose".

Since these challenges take place in sequential order, it should not be surprising to see that the qualities of "Fidelity", "Love", "Care" and "Wisdom" cannot be attained by those who have yet to master "Hope", "Will", "Purpose" and "Competence".

Hence, if one is seeking meaning in life, one should seek responsibility. Likewise if one is seeking motivation or will, one should seek to understand how and when to interact with the environment. If one is seeking hope one should seek out trust. If one has no one to trust they will feel hopeless, if one does not have a clear picture of what they need to be doing, one will feel lethargic, and if one has no responsibilities they have no meaning.

Stages of Moral Development (Kohlberg[35])

Stage	Thought Process
1	How can I avoid punishment?
2	What's in it for me?
3	It's right because society says so
4	It's right because the law says so
5	It's right because I owe that to society
6	Universal Moral Obligation

Kohlberg believed that as individuals mature, so does their moral reasoning. At first the individual is entirely selfish; the only deterrent for unethical behavior is fear of punishment. As the individual matures, unethical conduct is only prevented by the promise of a reward. As the individual matures further, ethical rather than unethical conduct is chosen, in order to conform to society. Moving along, the attitude changes and the focus shifts into doing what the law book says. The next step involves the individual choosing the correct behavior, because he/she feels that there is an obligation towards society. This is not motivated by the desire to conform, but rather by the desire to shape society. Finally the individual chooses the moral behavior, simply because it is moral to do so. The individual feels an obligation towards him/herself, and would do the same regardless of society.

[35] Moral stages and moralization: The cognitive-developmental approach, Moral Development and Behavior: Theory, Research and Social Issues. Kohlberg, Lawrence; T. Lickona, ed. (1976), Holt, NY: Rinehart and Winston. (See Wikipedia)

Stages of Development (Loevinger[36])

Stage	Thought Process
1	Impulsive - Egocentric - Body Senses
2	Self-Protective - Opportunistic - Control
3	Conformist - Respect for Rules - Appearance
4	Self-aware - Exceptions for rules - Adjustment
5	Conscientious - Self Evaluated - Achievements
6	Individualistic - Tolerant - Development
7	Autonomous - Coping with Conflict - Self Fulfilment
8	Integrated - Cherishing Individuality

According to Loevinger, infants start out their lives learning from sensory-motor inputs/outputs; there is little to no self-control and the behaviour is impulsive. As the child grows and gains control, the child becomes self-protective and seeks to control the environment. The next level involves a higher order of thinking, whereby the child learns to control urges and impulses which do not conform to the rules. Moving along, the individual becomes self-aware and understands that although there may be rules, there are also exceptions to those rules. Next, the individual realizes that he/she must evaluate his/her own behaviour regardless of what rules may or may not exist. Once the prior stage is complete the individual becomes an entity in its own right. It is at this stage that a human being can really be referred to as an individual. Once the individual has attained comfort with his/herself, the individual becomes autonomous and driven to self-actualise.

[36] Characteristics of Stages pp 5 Table 1.1

Finally the individual becomes fully integrated remaining as an individual but playing a role within society.

Based on the work of Erikson, Kohlberg and Loevinger, we can see that a large number of individuals are "stuck" in conformist, rule-based existence. It is no wonder why we see intolerance and discrimination within society.

It would appear that society at large is lacking in emotional and moral development, and has thus become fixated on rules and appearance, rather than on development leading to individuality, peace and wisdom.

If this lack took the form of physical developmental stagnation, we would have a society where the average height would be 50 centimetres, or 20 inches. It is truly sad to see, that a species as great as the human being has become nothing more than a consumer of materials. We will come back to this topic a little later.

The role of the Soul:

The Soul of the human being can be said to be fully mature. Given what we have stated above, this would mean that the Soul is:

1. Integrated
2. Cherishes individuality
3. Is bound by Universal Moral Obligation
4. Wisdom

The job of the Soul is to interact with the human mind in order for the human mind to interact with the human body. The ultimate goal is for all three parts, namely the body, mind and Soul, to be fully integrated and synchronised, in order to facilitate total self-control which is utilised for the benefit of the entire human species.

When the Soul enters the human body, the struggle begins as the Soul learns to operate the "Brain - Operating System" much like the learning curve when learning how to operate any new device. At first the movements are clumsy, but soon we get the hang of it.

As the brain matures, it becomes increasingly difficult for the Soul to "control" the body, and must begin developing a working partnership with the brain in order to reach the ultimate goal of self-actualisation.

For some, a partnership or friendship between the brain and the Soul is never developed, because of choices or otherwise. These individuals then become emotionally and morally "stuck" and develop no further. The Soul uses the emotions of an individual to communicate; however, when the emotions have been shut down, the line of communication becomes severed.

When we open ourselves up to emotion and experience, our Soul will naturally drive us to self-actualisation and we become wholesome in turn. We become seekers of wisdom and unique individuals, and in turn we become Super-Patient, expecting nothing from this planet. Our focus shifts from the low perspective of "what can I expect out of life?", to the higher perspective of "what does life expect of me?".

We seldom get it right the first time, and so, as we enter into this human body so we exit, and try again and again.

Infant	**Geriatric**
Trouble Walking	Trouble Walking
Trouble Seeing	Trouble Seeing
Trouble with controlling urination etc.	Trouble with controlling urination etc.
Trouble speaking clearly	Trouble speaking clearly
Sleeps a lot	Sleeps a lot

Happiness is a process not a thing:

The goal of being alive is to live honorably and with integrity. As we have seen above, the goal of life is not simply to have a good time, but rather to become a good person.

- You may have a good time, becoming a good person, but in most instances, you won't.
- You may become a good person, having a good time, but in most instances, you won't.

Since becoming a good person is a difficult task, many opt for the path of laziness and seek a good time instead of becoming a good person, and ultimately achieve nothing more than a troubled inner self.

As Aristotle wrote in his work Nicomachean Ethics[37], the definition of happiness is reached by studying the characteristic functioning of man. If we lose sight of the goal, we move further away from what we seek.

Every human being that has lived on planet Earth since its inception, has had one primary goal; namely to achieve a state of "Happiness". We are fully aware that we want happiness but we are unsure of how to get it.

- We know what we want, but we don't know where and how to get it.

1. We may chase after or utilise methods that we perceive will bring us "Happiness" and then fail.

[37] The Nicomachean Ethics, Aristotle, 230 BCE

2. We may focus on what we perceive to be causing us unhappiness and then seek to remove it, in an attempt to gain "Happiness".

3. If that fails, we may look for those things which bring us joy and try to increase them, only to realize that joy, excitement and pleasure are emotions and not "Happiness".

The first step in attaining "Happiness" is to realize that happiness is a process not a "Thing". In our world of material consumption, we are conditioned to believe that we must get as many things as possible, and so "Happiness" is on the list of things to acquire.

The most common mistake made, is that if we have enough "Things" then "Happiness" will be included, or manifest amongst those "Things". This reasoning assumes that if one was to purchase every "Thing" that exists, then somewhere amongst those "Things" will be the "Thing" called "Happiness".

- We try and acquire every "Thing" only to find that we have no "Thing".

To use an analogy, say one was looking to own the ultimate sports car, but had no idea of the make and model, they would go to the car dealer and say, "give me one of each", in the hope that somewhere in his/her collection of cars, would be the ultimate sports car. Even if he/she owns the ultimate sports car now, he/she will be unable to identify which one it is.

Important questions to ask:

1. Do I already have happiness, but cannot identify it?

2. How do I know if I am happy or not?

Many popular works have been written, claiming that if you do "XYZ", you can have anything you want. This is simply not true, and rather than giving you false hope, the truth is that you will in all likelihood not get most of the things that you want. However this does not mean that you have to be unhappy.

On the contrary, try and get whatever it is that you want; if you understand that happiness is a process, the outcome of getting what you want will neither accelerate, nor deter you from happiness.

- The process of happiness occurs when an individual overcomes adversity and incorporates good virtues within him/herself in the process.

Happiness can be likened to one's blood pressure or pulse, the pressure or pulse is a function of movement and not an entity within itself.

- Failure to overcome adversity stops the process of "Happiness".

You have not failed until you stop trying. Thus the process is activated and controlled by your effort. You choose when it starts i.e. when you identify an adversity to tackle, and you choose when it stops, i.e. when you no longer wish to tackle the adversity.

- Failure to incorporate good virtues stops the process of "Happiness".

If a positive character trait does not develop as a result of the adversity, happiness will stop flowing.

True happiness is one of the most difficult challenges a human being can encounter. It would be easier to jog up Mount Everest in a day, than to attain true happiness in its purest form[38]. For this reason, I have written a separate work dealing exclusively with happiness and positive thinking.

Genuine interest:

The Soul of the human being desires to be cared for. This means that as human beings we wish to be something significant in the life of another. This is not the desire for social acceptance, but rather a desire to have someone take a genuine interest in our development and well-being.

As children, we turn towards our parents, as we develop we turn towards our friends, spouses/partners and colleagues; when we mature, we turn towards ourselves or a higher power.

As human beings we would like to know, that someone cares if we are doing well or not. We would like to be assured that should something bad happen, someone will genuinely care and seek to resolve the issue together with us. Human beings want to feel that they matter.

All too often, we learn from life experience that we may not matter, or that there is no other, who genuinely cares for our well-being. This often results in a feeling of sadness or despair. In reality, many individuals delude themselves into thinking that there is someone who genuinely cares for their well-being, only to discover that in a time of crises, they stand alone.

Social media helps individuals to delude themselves into thinking that they matter, or that they have vast support networks. In reality, however there is always only a handful at most, of individuals who genuinely care for the well-being of another individual.

[38] See above - Three types of Human Beings that can tolerate Planet Earth

Important questions to ask:

1. If I were in trouble, who do I have to turn to?
2. How confident am I that I will not stand alone in a time of crisis?
3. Who can I open up to completely, without fear or embarrassment?
4. Who do I share my worries with?

Upon reaching maturity, one becomes comfortable with the idea, that your well-being is only your own concern. It is only you that genuinely cares whether you are doing well or not.

As the great sage Hillel said[39]:

"If I; am not for myself; who is for me? And if I am only for myself, then what am I?"

The idea is as follows: despite knowing that only you have a genuine interest in your own wellbeing, what are you if you only have an interest in your own wellbeing? Are you anything more than a selfish individual?

Thus the human being feels a sense of happiness when he/she is both significant in the life of another, and is in turn the holder of significance for another.

Thus, a great sense of unhappiness comes from not being significant to yourself, or not being significant to another.

Social conformists often devalue or value themselves based on the opinions of others. However, it is important to note that your own worth should never be placed in the hands of another individual.

[39] Ovos 1:14

Placing your own worth in the hands of another individual is tantamount to placing your banking passwords in a public space.

Your most precious asset, no matter how wealthy or poor you are, is your self-esteem. Ensure that you look after it, and protect it more than any other asset. It is always amusing to see an individual, who has vast sums of wealth, and protects his/her assets with the utmost diligence, and yet has simultaneously placed his/her self-esteem in the hands of another.

Inner and outer peace:

Along with the process of happiness that we seek, is the desire for inner peace. When we refer to inner peace we must first define its meaning, and differentiate it from outer peace.

- Inner peace refers to calmness of the mind, the opposite of anxiety. It is associated with clear thought, tranquility and concentration.

- Outer peace refers to relationships between the self and others. It is associated with loving relationships, cooperation and mutual understanding between two or more individuals.

"Inner peace" precedes "Outer peace" both in priority and in feasibility. Although "Happiness" is closely related to "Inner Peace", the two are mutually exclusive.

Maslow's hierarchy of needs:

The order of needs is as follows: (in ascending order)

1. Physiological needs - Including water, food, and shelter etc.

2. Safety needs - Once an individual has taken care of the basic survival requirements, the next step is to ensure the safety and well-being of people and possessions.

3. Love and belonging - Once an individual has taken care of the safety requirements, the attention of the individual shifts, to wanting love and belonging.

4. Esteem - Once an individual has found love and belonging, the individual develops a need to feel a sense of worth.

5. Self-actualisation - Once an individual has a sense of worth, the individual then develops a desire to reach their full potential.

You may notice that there is a gap between step 2 and step 3, whereby the individual shifts his/her attention from material needs to psychological needs. This model thus requires further clarification.

The true hierarchy of needs:

Although Maslow only speaks of "love and belonging at stage 3, these desires are present simultaneous, to the basic desire of physical survival. As we have seen above, love and belonging are essential components to happiness. It would be incorrect to assume that one who is seeking basic survival, no longer wants to be loved and belong. On the contrary one who lacks the most basic of necessities has an even stronger desire for love, belonging and esteem.

Because human beings are made up of three core elements, the desire emanating from each element is always present. What we focus on, however may form a hierarchy.

Likewise, although Maslow only speaks of lofty desires at stage 5, the desires of the Soul are also present simultaneous, to the psychological and physical desires.

Thus, the more one can stabilise, secure and maintain the systems of needs, the more content one can feel. Feeling content for prolonged periods of time, brings happiness in turn.

6

ONTOLOGY – ABSOLUTE VERSUS PERCEIVED REALITY

The word ontology is seldom used outside of scholastic circles, yet its application and relevance is every bit as important to the scholar as it is to the layman.

If you have never heard of the word, ontology, don't be ashamed. I too was using ontology from the age of eight, but had no idea such a word even existed until my mid-twenties.

For many years, I have been fascinated by the inner workings of the mind; this in no small part pushed me in the academic direction of psychology. What fascinated me most was the fact that people can disagree.

What seemed obvious to everyone else seemed to puzzle me. I recall a time when I was eight years old, and I encountered two people arguing over some trivial matter. Each person was adamant they were right; others began taking sides and before long two groups emerged each staunchly holding their own views to be correct.

While I was standing and observing, I noticed the two groups were both correct. They were both misunderstanding each other, and talking about two different elements of the same item.

In reality, the item contained both elements. Group A was fixated on element A, whereas Group B was fixated on element B. As an eight-year-old; I had no place in setting the matter straight, but it left me with a sense of frustration, why couldn't Group A see Group B's point of view and vice versa?

By the age of eleven or so, I just accepted it as a matter of fact; some people are blind in their eyes, and some people are blind in their mind. Just as I couldn't explain the colour red to the physically blind, I also couldn't explain my thoughts and ideas to those who were mentally blind.

I tried for many years with absolutely zero success, to try and find a way of putting across the idea: that everybody is right, all the time, depending on their perspective, I was always met with skepticism, hostility and anger.

Finally, after fifteen years of study I came across the word ontology. This word was the one I had been looking for, for so many years.

So what is ontology? Ontology is the study of existence and reality. In not so many words ontology is the realisation that there are in fact many realities. Your perspective is just one of many vantage points from which to view. Closely related is the subject of epistemology which deals with our unique perspective, I will discuss epistemology shortly.

Armed with two words namely ontology and epistemology, I will now try once again to explain why nothing really exists and why your opinion or view is entirely insignificant in terms of the bigger picture.

I am almost certain that almost every conflict can be resolved with a basic understanding of what is being presented here.
To understand ontology we need to go back to the beginning, the point at which existence began. Based on what we have said previously, namely all which exists is merely a manifestation of the Creator, we will see at least two separate realities exist.

The absolute reality:
The absolute reality is that only the Creator is real and everything else is simply a complex illusion.

Many people have come to know this concept, but have not grasped its full magnitude.

- You are not real.
- The chair you are sitting on is not real.
- The food you are eating isn't real.
- Nothing around you is real.

The 1999 film, The Matrix, went along way to illustrate this concept. You needn't watch all the sequels, or read all the literature which has been produced discussing the film itself. The original film illustrated a concept, we are all plugged into a virtual reality. The virtual reality is so perfect and precise, it feels 100% real.

However, in the absolute reality only one thing exists, the Creator himself. It is for this reason that we say the Creator is one. The only being with objective reality is the Creator; absolutely everything else is a manifestation of the Creator, hence only one thing or Source has a real point of reality. Everything else obtains its reality in relation to that single point.

At the heart of creation, is a fundamental concept, that a singular being with objective reality, created other beings which have subjective or perceived realities.

Instead of asking where in the world the Creator is, we should be asking where in the Creator the world is.

The miracle of creation was not so much what the Creator made, but rather what he hid from our vision. If you want the ultimate virtual reality game, you are busy living in it. You have taken the bait, hook, line and sinker; so much so that the absolute reality is so absurd, it doesn't warrant any time or energy to investigate it further.

The best analogy I can use to explain this concept is that of fire. One flame can light another without diminishing the power of the first. The second flame in turn, has the same power as the first flame, and is thus capable of lighting yet another flame, all while leaving the first flame untouched. Each flame lit is a manifestation of the original flame and thus in absolute terms, there is only one flame burning at multiple locations.

Although this analogy is not perfect, it gives us an idea of what the term "One" or "Oneness" actually means.

Hence the source is one and everything else is a continuation of that original source. In our context, Source or the Creator is the first flame and every other item is a continuation of the original source.

The difference between our analogy and that of the Creator is that unlike the second flame, which can continue to exist without the first flame being present, in terms of the Creator all secondary items can only continue to exist if the Creator is present.

In order for the Creator to create this optical illusion, many steps of separation had to be created for the Creator to distance himself from the creation. If you look at the spiritual map, you will now begin to see why there is so much activity between the Creator in the realm of absolute reality, and our realm of perceived reality.

Perceived reality:
The perceived reality is that you are real. After all, can you not see, and feel all that is around you?

This is the default setting for the human being, in which the following holds true:

- You are real
- The chair you are sitting on is real.
- The food you are eating is real. (the label even says "made from real fruit")
- Everything around you is real.

Unlike The Matrix, both of these realities are true simultaneously, hence you do and don't exist all at the same time.

At first this seems like a contradiction, but it isn't, granted this is a difficult concept to grasp, and in all likelihood you will revert to the default setting of perceived reality. However if you do manage to grasp this concept fully it will humble you into complete silence.

For practical purposes, we live in a world of perceived reality. This means that what we deem to be real is very subjective and based entirely on our own perspective. This brings us to the concept of epistemology, the science of perception.

Every individual has a different perception of the world around him/herself. If the world population is currently seven billion people, we should say there are seven billion different ways in which to view the world.

Thus in any conflict, both or all parties are correct from their own vantage point. A vantage point which incorporates many other vantage points will be closer to the absolute reality, than a vantage point which does not include other points of view.

In summary, groups of people form when they view an element of reality from a single perspective. Conflict arises when two parties cannot incorporate another vantage point, and thus become fixated. Conflict resolution comes about where the parties concerned are able and willing to incorporate new vantage points.

In any event, it is always paramount to understand that a conflict arises in the realm of perceived reality, and not absolute reality. In the realm of absolute reality, a state of total equilibrium always exists.

7

GRADATION – LEVELS OF AWARENESS

Now that we have introduced the concept of epistemology, we can take this concept a little further.

Earlier we said that, if there are seven billion people in the world, then there are seven billion different ways to view the world. But what does that mean?

The human brain is a magnificent and complex organ. Every human being has their own brain, and every brain has its own "operating system".

To use the computer as an analogy: imagine your brain is the hardware component of a computer system, and that your perceptions and world views, are equivalent to an operating system, such as Windows, a software package that determines how the machine is to handle and process information.

Say you are running Windows 10, or let us call it "Braindows 10"; your one friend is running Linux, or "Brainux" and your other friend is running Android, or "Braindroid". Each one of you will see and interpret the same event in a different way.

Based on your brain's "software" each one of you will form a unique perspective. There are seven billion different operating systems for the brain, and every time someone is born, a new operating system is made. Therefore no two human beings are alike.

The way in which each operating system on a computer handles data, results in an entirely different look and feel, for each operating system. For example, Windows 95 looks different to Windows 2000, Windows XP, Windows Vista, Windows 7, Windows 8 and Windows 10[40].

Despite that all these operating systems are made by Microsoft, each has its own unique look and feel. The same is true for all the versions of Apple operating systems, Linux systems and Ubuntu systems.

Each human being has his/her own "software" running on his/her brain. In my work, Money Grows on Trees I delve into the topic of how this software can be installed and uninstalled.

However, for now it is sufficient to know, that although we can reach consensus on any topic or issue, say for example we agree the wall is painted red; neither of us are seeing the exact same thing. The red that I see may be different from the red that you see. Where the difference is subtle we choose to agree, but when the difference is large we tend to argue.

In reality, our epistemology or our "software" is processing sensory data inputs from our senses, and making sense of it all. Neither one of us has the true perspective, only a processed piece of information.

The "software" or epistemology of an individual may be faulty, and even when this "software" is working fine, the brain often fills in the gaps to help us make sense of the sensory input.

[40] These are contemporary examples; newer examples will be needed in the future.

We see with our brain:
Contrary to popular belief, we don't see with our eyes, but with our brains. The eye is merely a receptacle to receive light and turn that into electrical signals to be processed by the brain in the occipital lobe.

There are several principles of visual perception which often cause conflict between what we see and how our brains translate the sensory input. Sternberg (2009)[41] mentions six common errors which occur during the processing phase of visual inputs. I have included some illustrations which demonstrate this point.

How many planks do you see?
Your brain is trying to make sense of this image, but your eyes and brain are confused.

Which line is crooked?
Look at each line individually and each one appears to be straight.

[41] Cognitive Psychology, 5th edition, Robert J Sternberg, Wadsworth, USA pp 94

What do you see? Faces, a candle stick or both?

There are of course many more illustrations which cause visual perception errors. The same holds true for all of our senses. As human beings, our senses are not to be trusted, as they are fallible and prone to error.

This leads us to the conclusion that in absolute terms, we actually know nothing about anything, and we have no idea what is and isn't real.

This idea is a hard pill to swallow, especially for those who are absolutely confident. In truth, the more you know, the more you learn how little you really know.

On a practical level, we need to operate and function. For this reason it is important to be aware of gradation - a spectrum of possibilities, as well as levels of awareness - a series of progressions.

Gradation:
It is important for us to think of our knowledge as a "volume control" rather than an "on/off" switch. The volume control is graded, meaning it has several points along a spectrum of possibilities, ranging from the minimum amount to the maximum amount. The on/off switch has only two possible states of being either on or off.

So too with our knowledge, opinions, views and perceptions, we should be aware that we may know a little about something, or a lot about something. However we never know everything.

You will never hear a wise person say, they are 100% sure that what they are saying is correct. You will however find a wise person saying he/she is 99% sure, as this connotes both a degree of confidence as well as the realisation of the fallibility of the human condition.

It is this 1% of "darkness", which allows doubt to exist in the first place. This is the Achilles heel of the human mind, and precisely what the Creator warned Adam about[42]. If not for this weakness, it would be impossible for a person to have any negative thoughts or feelings. Thus the Creator warned Adam, that doubt combined with knowledge is a fatal combination. When approaching the Creator using one's intellect (complex-faith), it is vital to be aware of this blind-spot, in our faculty of logic.

Levels of awareness:
One of the greatest stumbling blocks is that to date, we have no concrete definition of consciousness. The question "What is consciousness?" sometimes referred to as the "hard problem" has no definitive answer.

To understand the hard problem, let us understand the following: we all agree that regardless of gender, culture or ethnicity, we all experience. That means to say we feel ourselves being alive, feeling our surroundings and feeling a sense of self. We all agree that when one is unconscious, such as when under anaesthetic, one does not experience

[42] Genesis 2:17 – The tree of knowledge

or feel one's surroundings or sense of self. When we are "on" we call this being conscious, and when we are "off" we call this being unconscious. However what exactly is the cause of us having this feeling of existence?

To understand this concept, we need to appreciate the fact that consciousness must be understood from the paradigm of gradation. Consciousness is not an on/off switch, but rather has various degrees to which one can experience it.

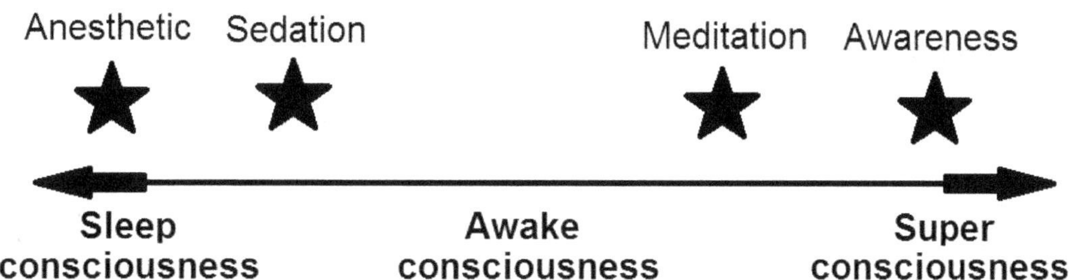

I would state that what is commonly referred to as consciousness, is better defined as "awake consciousness". This means that when we are awake, we are experiencing the world, on one level of consciousness.
If we mark four points along the continuum of consciousness, we can elaborate as follows: when one is under anaesthetic one cannot feel or sense physical sensations. When one is sedated one's senses are dulled, and we have a limited sense of physical sensations. When one is awake, one is able to feel physical sensations. When one meditates, one can sense more than physical sensations, and when one is super conscious, one can become "aware" or sense all which is possible for a human being to experience.

True awareness will only occur at death. However during life; and during waking moments we continuously fluctuate along the consciousness spectrum.
One could speculate that the reason we always revert back to awake consciousness, or below, is due to the fact that we are simply avoiding pain.

8

MULTIPLE VIEWS – UNIVERSAL VERSUS GRANULAR VIEW

Perception and delusion:

Everything which can be perceived by the human mind is subject to the law of multiple views. A concept can be viewed from a global or universal perspective, looking at the bigger picture, on the one hand, or viewing a concept in more subtle detail, looking at particular nuances, which is the granular perspective.

The realities which emerge from these two perspectives often give rise to conflict, or inconsistency. However, both set of truths are in fact true, simultaneously and contradictory to one another[43]. This can be demonstrated with Newton's laws of physics which are correct on one level of perception, but are not applicable on the quantum level.

Both Newton's laws of motion and the laws of quantum physics are true simultaneously and contradictory to one another.

Many great authors such as Richard Dawkins and Sam Harris have written extensively and eloquently about the concept of delusion.

[43] See further on: the topic of Islam as a religion.

The basic premise revolves around the concept that believing in a Creator or any other item for that matter, without hard evidence is simply delusional and non-scientific. This premise is most certainly valid.

While both Richard Dawkins and Sam Harris among others, are intellectually honest in their approach, and make sound rational arguments, which is noteworthy and admirable, as they care enough to engage in a rational manner, unlike many theists who resort to irrationality and faulty logic, when confronted with difficult concepts, both Richard Dawkins and Sam Harris are consistent in their views and maintain a rational disposition, something which all theists ought to do.

However, there remains yet another point of view which one needs to address, in order to understand the concept of the Creator, beyond the childlike narrative so many believers adhere to.

If one wants to understand the Creator in a mature way, one needs the following criteria:

1. One must care enough to investigate this matter with commitment and dedication. This means to say, one must view the search for the Creator as a matter which is no less important than investigating a crime scene. Laziness is no substitute for reasoning.

If one views the search for the Creator as a trivial matter, subject to whims and opinions, and less important than say, your bank statements, or your job for example, you are not a serious searcher.
On this point, I truly admire Richard Dawkins and Sam Harris for their sincere contributions. In my mind, these individuals are spiritual leaders in the sense that they have addressed the philosophical issues in a mature and eloquent manner.

2. One needs to be intellectually honest. This means to say that, rather than resorting to irrational thinking or delusional ideas, one must remain perfectly rational.

It is far better to say, "I don't know the answer", than to resort to irrational ideas to support your particular belief system. Emotive persuasions are no substitute for critical thinking.

Once again Richard Dawkins and Sam Harris are intellectually honest, and do not resort to irrationality when confronted with challenges. I would even go as far to say that reading their works is an excellent starting point for anyone wishing to develop a mature and rational understanding of the nature of the Creator. Their respective works clear the congestive minds of the irrational believer.

3. The third criterion, which is perhaps the most important, is a paradigm shift relating to the concept of understanding.

- The childish mindset says things like "They can't all be right, which one is the real one?" or, "My views are correct, while yours are incorrect".

- The adult mindset on the other hand says things like "If they are all right, how do we reconcile the following?" or, "If both our views are correct, then what is lacking in our global perspective?"

It is at this point that many great scholars fail, and ultimately draw the wrong conclusion about the nature of reality, and the nature of the Creator.

If your belief in the Creator is based on irrational thought, and false arguments, then you are in fact delusional, and your beliefs are fickle and unfounded.

If your beliefs are based on sound logic and deep understanding however, you will clearly see that no "tricks" are needed, in order to believe in the Creator using complex faith. Your beliefs don't have to be overly complex, but they should be able to withstand a degree of scrutiny.

In addition a belief based on reason can withstand any questioning with absolute confidence. It is imperative that the theist remains a critical thinker at all times. Searching for the Creator as a mature adult is not a hobby or pastime, but rather a full time occupation, requiring every faculty of one's being at all times.

Multiple views:

A = 1 Item

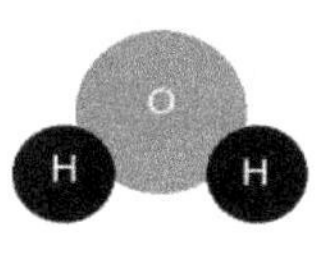

B = Billions of Items

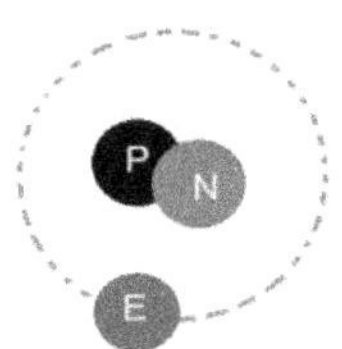

C = Hundreds of Trillions of Items

In the diagram above, we have item "A" a cup of water. There is only one cup of water, therefore it would be correct and truthful to say, in front of you lays one item.

However the cup of water contains water after all, and we know a water molecule is made up of one Oxygen atom and two Hydrogen atoms.

On an atomic level, it is truthful to say that in front of you lay billions of items, namely atoms. Going one step further, we know atoms are made up of even smaller particles such as protons, neutrons and electrons, thus on a sub atomic level, it is truthful to say that in front of you lay hundreds of trillions of items.

We need not go further into the sub-atomic anatomy of quarks, and possibly ending in strings of matter. The point to bear in mind is that, what appears as one item from a universal perspective, is in actual fact multiple items, when viewed at the granular level or from the granular perspective.

The universal perspective is just as true as the granular perspective, hence multiple truths co-exists, while seeming to contradict one another.

The argument will revolve around how many items lay in front of you; one individual may say "one item", while another may say "hundreds of trillions of items". They are both in fact correct.

When we deeply examine any topic or concept, we must appreciate the universal perspective versus the granular perspective. One can never know the full truth of any topic unless one fully understands the beginning, the middle and the end.

Using our cup of water analogy above; in order to have a holistic truthful answer, one must know the exact size of the universe, as well as the smallest particle. This will yield a beginning and an end, which is the starting point. Next, we would then analyse the perceived middle, namely the cup of water.

Once we have a starting point, and an ending point, we will then be in a better position to judge which option of either "one item" or "hundreds of trillions of items" is a better descriptor.

However to fixate on a single variable, is to miss the point entirely. Truth is not something which is created; it is found through widening the perspective of observation. Truth stands on its own, and can be recognised easily. If we are honest with ourselves we can easily spot the truth.

The question: "Is there a Creator or not?" is a question incumbent on every individual to ask, even if left unanswered.

This is perhaps the best question any human being can and should ask. Failure to ask this question is tantamount to failure in life itself. The answer to this question is irrelevant, merely asking the question and expanding your mind will provide more meaning and depth, than any single answer can ever provide, be it true or false.

One, who is seeking truth, is one that is always searching. To stop searching, is to stop seeking the truth. If the Creator has not cropped up on your "radar", then your search parameters are too small.

Both the atheist and the theist have asked the all-important question. Both are looking for satisfactory answers which will appease the rational mind. There is nothing more frustrating to the human mind than not having an answer to a question. As I have stated numerous times however, a good question is better than an unsatisfactory answer.

Good questions lead to great discoveries along the way, while answers produce stagnation.

If you want to discover what is in the room, don't peep through the keyhole, open the door and look inside.

At this point you will have come to the realisation that the creation is complex and that we are fallible in nature.

I hope that you have begun to see the greatness of the Creator, and found a reason to love and please the Creator.

This complexity is the source of both good and bad. The good element is that it opens your eyes to the wonders of the Creator, however knowing this complexity can make you doubt yourself and everything you know, and it is this doubt which often traps people.

This is precisely what happened to Adam - the first man. Adam had simple faith and could not be harmed. Once he ate from the tree of knowledge however, he became aware of complexity.

Complexity is very powerful, it can build and destroy. The "Snake" used this tool to make Adam doubt the truth which he knew so clearly. Unfortunately the atheist gets deluded by the "snake of complexity".

There are two options:

1. We can either adopt **simple faith** - meaning that we connect to the Creator from a place of emotion (recommended setting).
2. We can adopt **complex faith** - meaning that we connect to the Creator from a place of logic. (For advanced users)

The atheist gets deluded by the "snake of complexity"

Ideally we should be able to maintain both simple and complex faith, however this is a level which requires heavy lifting, and is not for the faint hearted.

9

KEEPING IT REAL

MODERATION AND PACE

At this point in the book, we have spoken about the concepts of multiple realities, levels of awareness and the universal verses the granular perspectives.

In a sense we have just learnt about the steering wheel, the accelerator and the brakes of our "vehicle" which we use to journey through life. We have spoken about the instrumentation but we have not yet spoken about, how to use these instruments.

In this section we will look at, when and how to use this instrumentation. Imagine the following scenario: Tiffany is a 42 year old micro biologist; she spends almost 8 hours a day, every day of the week, peering down the lenses of an electron microscope, analyzing bacteria. Her occupation has primed her, to view the world in miniature. On a daily basis Tiffany deals only with that which cannot be seen by the naked eye. Tiny items for her are a big deal in her occupational world. Yet at the end of each working day Tiffany gets into her car and drives the two hour long commute back home. Tiffany is a great driver, in the last 22 years she has never once had an accident.

She pays attention to the road signs and is constantly vigilant about the traffic that surrounds her on her daily commute.

Although Tiffany spends all day peering down the microscope, she is able to adjust her eye sight from the micro-world to the macro-world with ease. Tiffany has successfully shifted from two perspectives; she has learnt how to adjust to the demands required of her in each situation.

In our daily commute in the journey of life, we too need to acquire the skills needed to adjust to the various demands placed on us in various situations.

Let us summarize the concepts as follows:

1. Absolute versus perceived reality: This control allows us to engage and disengage, from the world around us.
2. Levels of awareness: This control allows us to feel the sensations to varying degrees when we are engaged.
3. Universal versus granular perspective: This control allows us to zoom in and zoom out, whilst we experience the world around us.

There are times when one should engage, and there are times where it is more appropriate to disengage. Likewise there are times where one should feel the sensations of being alive in the present moment, and there are other times where it is more appropriate not to feel the sensations of the present moment. So too there are times when one needs to zoom in, and there are times when one needs to zoom out.

It is quite obvious that during open heart surgery, it would make more sense to not feel the physical sensations of being operated on. Likewise it would make more sense to look for stars in the night sky using a telescope rather than a microscope. However beyond the common sense application of this principle, we need the knowledge of when to apply the other controls of perception, and to what degree.

As a golden rule moderation and pace produce the best results in the long run. If we take food as an example; Chocolate is absolutely fine in moderation, but a diet consisting of nothing but chocolate will lead to weight gain and a lack of general wellbeing.

Using a marathon as an example, the old dictum "Slow and steady wins the race" is very true. Trying to make many drastic changes in one's life in a short period of time, will inevitability lead to failure in all areas of one's life.

Thus one should never become "stuck" in one perception, and at the same time one's perceptions should not be so fluid that one is unable to function on a daily basis.

Just as the airplane pilot needs to configure his/her aircraft for takeoff and landing, so too one must configure his/her mind with the appropriate settings when approaching the Creator.

The appropriate settings include:

1. Disengagement set to maximum.
2. Awareness set to maximum
3. Universal perspective set to maximum.

In order to begin a search of this nature, one must be able to disconnect from all that is physical, however one needs to be fully aware of all physical sensations, and one must be open to the universal perspective.

It goes without saying that setting up the right configuration, is different for each individual as each individual has unique properties which will either allow or restrain the ultimate settings. For example one who is suffering physical or emotional pain may find it very difficult to set their awareness level to maximum, as this may enhance the sensation of pain, which in turn disturbs and distorts other faculties of the mind.

The ideal head-space to be in, in order to configure the mind correctly is one in which one has no hold-ups with letting go of all of his/her perceived ideas.

Therefore the ideal environment is one which supports unconditional love and acceptance. Similarly unless one possesses great fortitude it will be close to impossible to meditate or reach higher levels of awareness.

Lastly one who is tied down by a purely physical understanding of existence will struggle with the concept of the universal perspective, as the broadness of the cosmos will no doubt make this individual feel entirely insignificant, which will leave the individual feeling deflated and desponded. This in turn can lead to feelings of hopelessness and even depression.

Just as the polar bear strives in extremely cold climates, and the camel strives in extremely hot climates. We too need to find our ideal habitat where we can freely express ourselves without any hindrance or set back. If we are like the polar bear that is stuck in the dessert, we will be completely at loss to search and find the Creator.

Hence we should seek out the best and most suitable surroundings that allow our mind to wonder in a free and unhindered way.

Granted the Utopian conditions are exceptionally hard to find, however when one looks and moves with a sense of purpose, one will find that even the non-ideal situation can lead to the maximum yield. Ultimately one must make do with the resources available to him/her. Sometimes the most challenging life situations present opportunities which would not arise in a regular daily routine.

Keeping it real:

So long as one is open-minded and is able to utilize some of the tools that we have spoken about, it should not be difficult to see the world from multiple perspectives.

You don't have to agree with another person's perspective; you just need to understand why that particular person holds that perspective to be true.

Who is wise? One who learns from every person[44]...

Each and every person has a unique perspective, the more one understands different world views the more one is able to co-exist with others.

It may not be possible to love every person as you do yourself, as that is a tall order for all but the most saintly individuals. However one, who is sincere about understanding the many complexities of the universe, will be intellectually honest with both him/her self and with others.

Keeping it real or being sincere is about being rational and critical of one's own beliefs and opinions.

You may aspire to wholeheartedly love the human race, but that will not happen overnight, nor will it happen without consistent hard work and relentless dedication. The fullness of the human condition cannot be attained by chance.

Just as no one is born an Olympic athlete, or expert neuro-surgeon, no one is born with the character traits needed, to be the ideal human being. Everything which is lasting, meaningful and worthwhile takes years of diligent practice and countless instances of trial and error.

[44] Ovos 4:1

Becoming the ultimate version of you will take no less than a life time to accomplish. The ultimate version of you is all that is required, nothing more and nothing less. Don't try and become the ultimate version of somebody else, not only will you fail, but you will find absolutely no fulfillment in that endeavor.

I've got it covered – False reassurance

Human beings have a tendency to safeguard and protect all that which is important. Although we like to think that human beings are rational beings, many studies[45] show that human beings make their choices based more on emotions than they do on pure rational thinking.

Perhaps the most important emotion that drives the actions of a human being is the emotion of hope. Hope is so powerful, to the point that a human being can hardly function without it. A human being in a state of hopelessness is so far removed from life, that one can hardly call that being a living being. One might go as far as to say that hope is the most valuable asset which a human being can possess.

Is hope rational?

Imagine that you were on an airplane, which crashed on some remote island, and that you and a handful of other passengers were the only survivors. After 72 hours your chances of being rescued alive fall dramatically, statistically speaking the odds are against you making it out alive. If you were purely rational, you should give up hope and simply accept your fate of imminent death, and yet against the odds you irrationally cling to the emotion of hope, you push on, one day at a time in the hope that you will eventually be rescued alive. Hope is sometimes completely irrational and yet our very survival depends on it.

[45] The upside of irrationality Dan Ariely, Harper Perennial, 2011

When it comes to life, as well as the afterlife, we all hope and believe that things will work out in the end and that everything is going to be ok.

We are aware that along the way we may lose things which are important to us, and we try as best we can, to protect everything which we feel is valuable. It is for this reason that we like to purchase insurance, for we know that should something unforeseen happen we have it covered. We feel safer, and perhaps happier with the thought that "I've got it covered". Knowing that you can minimize your losses is very reassuring. With this reassurance we take on bigger risks and we dare ourselves to live life to its fullest.

For many individuals, spirituality and/or religion are forms of insurance.

- If my car is stolen, I'm covered, I have car insurance.
- If my house burns down, I'm covered, I have home insurance.
- If I become disabled or die, I'm covered; I have life and disability insurance.
- After I die, I'm covered, I have "INSERT YOUR DEITY HERE"

Religious individuals are particularly prone to this type of false reassurance, when it comes to the afterlife. How often do we see and hear religious individuals assure themselves that after they die they will certainly go to heaven or paradise because they believed in "INSERT YOUR DEITY HERE"

This believe is simply a hope, and as we have seen above hope is not rational. Rational thinking dictates that if one is to search for the Creator, then at least 2 distinct possibilities exist.

1. There is no Creator
2. There is a Creator

Several religions, which base their beliefs in sacred texts, make the claim that one who does XYZ is guaranteed an afterlife of bliss for all eternity.

However without:

1. An open mind.
2. A desire for the ultimate truth.
3. A personal life journey.
4. Honesty with oneself.

One should be acutely aware that, as tempting as the guarantee sounds, that may not be what you discover.

If the truth reveals itself to be, that there is one Creator, who is in fact cruel and merciless

- Are you prepared to accept that?
- Are you prepared to discover something which you may not like?
- Are you prepared to live your life, knowing that there is only one service provider?

If there is a Creator, and if there is only one, you will have to accept that truth. Unlike your internet service provider whom you can change at any time, when you feel that you are not getting the service you desire, if there is only one service provider for spirituality, you are compelled to use it regardless of your sentiments.

In the search for the Creator, one must be ready and willing to accept, whatever the results may yield regardless of whether or not it makes you feel better or worse. Like a scientific experiment one must ask the right research questions, one must conduct scholarly research and one must report accurate outcomes.

In order to do this, one ought to place ones ego and sentiments to the side, perhaps your search will lead to satisfactory conclusions, which will be both accurate and appealing. However drawing conclusions without asking questions and doing scholarly research is the domain of small children and immature adults.

My personal journey has led me to conclude that there is a Creator, who is loving and compassionate. My awareness was given to me as a gift from heaven, despite my many shortcomings.

Go ahead and take your own journey...

Obstacles

"My poverty is a witness to my honesty"
Niccolo Machiavelli

Disclaimer: The following section contains material which some readers may find offensive.

Its purpose; is for none other than to help those in search of the Creator. Therefore no truth has been spared.

Reader discretion is advised.

The purpose of the upcoming section is not to offend any culture, gender, race, religion or sexual orientation, but rather to prepare the reader for the tasks of acting like the Creator, and having pure intentions.

Unfortunately, due to misinformation spread over thousands of years, many individuals have become confused, and need to be reminded of the truth. The next few chapters are based on opinion, through observation and research. The assertions made are in no way intended to cause harm to any individual, in any capacity whatsoever. I will address topics in the broadest way possible, and in a manner that is fair and balanced.

I therefore need to make the reader aware of various obstacles that interfere with the relationship between man and his creator.

May the light of the Creator, shine on us all, so that there is everlasting peace, in the world.

10
RELIGIONS OF THE WORLD

Contrary to popular belief, religion or modern day organized religion specifically, is one of the greatest obstacles impeding the search of, and the connection to, the Creator.

The adherents of a particular organised religion are often led to complacency and rote, in which the very concept of the Creator is lost within the tasks and duties of the religion itself.

For some weak-minded individuals, who either lack critical thinking skills, self-governance skills, or emotional intelligence, religion can be a wonderful tool.

It is not uncommon for a religion to transform an otherwise reckless human being, into a purposeful individual, as is the case with many individuals, who find purpose and meaning within the confines of the prison environment, through association with a particular faith or religion.

The term "religion" is simply an English word in the dictionary, it is not a term used by the Creator. We need to gain an understanding of what an organised religion actually is, and why this hinders spiritual growth.

To begin it is important to note some of the key concepts pertaining to religion:

- Some religions are entirely faith-based, meaning an individual becomes integrated into that particular religious group based entirely on a set of shared principles or beliefs. Other religions are based on a particular bloodline, meaning an individual becomes integrated into that particular religious group based entirely on ancestry, regardless of that individual's beliefs.

As an example:

A. Islam is a faith-based religion. In order to be a Muslim one must accept Allah as the one and only God, and Muhammad as the perfect prophet, whose life and behaviour is to be emulated in all ways. One cannot be an atheist Muslim, since Islam dictates which beliefs an individual must have in order to be classified as a Muslim. Likewise, a Muslim who does not emulate the prophet Muhammad is not a true Muslim.

B. On the other hand, Judaism is a bloodline religion. In order to be classified as a Jew; an individual must have a Jewish mother. Thus one can have an atheist Jew, i.e. one who is born from a Jewish mother, but does not believe in God. Likewise, one who is born from a Jewish mother is classified as a Jew, even if that individual does not practice the Jewish religion.

- In every religion, the religious group itself can be split into two groups, one group being scholars of that religion, who actively study and understand their religion, and the second group being those who have very little knowledge and understanding of their own religion.

It would be difficult to put a number to this divide, but let us assume that the split is 90/10, meaning only 10% of any religious sect comprises of scholars, while the other 90% are not intimately familiar with the religion they ascribe to.

As an example, using the Abrahamic religions:

- ❖ 90% of Christians have not studied the Old Testament in Hebrew and the New Testament in ancient Greek, the original format in which they were written.
- ❖ 90% of Jews have not studied the written and Oral Torah in Hebrew and Aramaic, the original format in which they were written.
- ❖ 90% of Muslims have not studied the Quran, Hadith and Sira in Arabic the original format in which they were written.

Bearing the above in mind, observing the behaviors of a Christian, Jew or Muslim is a very poor indicator of what that religion is all about.

In order to understand any religion, one must examine the doctrine and literature of that particular religion. One needs to be a scholar before declaring allegiance to a particular religion. Unfortunately too few individuals take their faith seriously enough, to pursue the undertaking of scholarly research, and instead opt for the lazy alternative, of observing others of the same faith, and mimicking their behaviours.

The scholars amongst a religious group, who take their faith seriously, are better equipped to find the Creator on an intellectual level using complex faith. The unlearned have to rely on simple faith, or else they may be caught up in the river of organised religion, being guided by anyone and everyone, and having no knowledge of their own.

This does not mean to say that those who use simple faith are not learned. In fact the very opposite is true. Since the Creator desires our emotions over our intellect, only simple faith has the power to be emotionally charged.

In order to seek and find the Creator, one must classify him/herself as a "Truth Seeker" rather than a "religious" or "spiritual" individual. As a

"Truth-Seeker", one encompasses all that is true in all organised religions, and rejects all that is false in all organised religions.

To place a "Truth-Seeker" into a man-made religion is to place an elephant into a matchbox. A "Truth-Seeker" is beyond the limited scope of man-made constructs, and seeks the unlimited understanding of an infinite Creator. Nothing which is infinite can be contained within that which is finite.

The more abstract a concept, the more difficult it becomes to prove. For example, can I prove there is a difference between hate and anger?

The most abstract concept is that of the Creator. As we stated earlier, the Creator does not exist on a physical level, just as love does not exist on a physical level. Love does not occupy space and contains no matter, thus it does not exist.

To understand love, means to broaden one's mind, to allow the construct to be felt and experienced on a different level. So too, to understand the Creator, requires a broadening of the mind to allow for the abstract to be felt and experienced.

Finding the Creator within the boundaries of religion, would be the equivalent of me saying "I want you to love this person for exactly 23 minutes." If I love someone, I cannot possibly love them for just 23 minutes, as the emotion cannot be contained within the finite construct of time.

In summary:

First find the Creator, and then perform all the duties which the Creator has tasked you with. The obstacle lays within the word itself, try imagining that there was no name for your set of beliefs.

Organised Crime and Organised Religion

Organised religion, although often well intended, most often produces the worst possible outcome for its participants.

Organised religion is highly prone to producing zombie-like individuals. These individuals conduct themselves and go about their daily routine out of sheer habit, as if left to chance.

Moreover these individuals are entirely disengaged from life itself, acting without any forethought or rationality, and display themselves, as being almost entirely void of human emotion.

These individuals forego their identity and lose their personality, trying to conform to the said organised religion.

The dulling of the mind of these individuals, shuts down any possibility for introspection, and ultimately produces irrational and heartless human beings as a by-product.

Furthermore there is a more sinister aspect to organised religion; organised religion mimics organised crime in almost every way imaginable. By comparing the nature of organised crime and organised religion we will see that they are in fact one in the same thing.

The features of organised crime:

When one thinks of organised crime, images of mafia bosses like Al Capone spring to mind. Hollywood has glorified the shrewd and cunning masterminds who wield enormous power, and strike terror in the hearts of all who interrupt their dealings.

However, in reality organised crime, cripples growth and development, marginalises the poor, and gives a select handful of individuals' rights and privileges, the rest of us don't have.

In the world of organised crime:

1. There is an authority figure namely the boss or godfather.
2. The authority figure is usually dubious in nature, being narcissistic and maniacal.
3. The authority figure is a well-crafted social manipulator.
4. Those with a close relationship to the authority figure are given special privileges.
5. Entering the group requires an act of loyalty.
6. Leaving the group is almost impossible.
7. Lower ranking minions are left to do the dirty work, while higher-ranking minions enjoy privilege and status.
8. Nepotism is rife, with family occupying positions of power.
9. Questioning the authority figure is met with harsh consequences.
10. Those who are not a part of the group are treated as enemies.
11. Climbing the ranks requires unwavering loyalty to the authority figure.
12. The group conducts its affairs with blatant disregard for society as a whole.
13. The dealings and conduct of the group are secretive.
14. The group covers up its unlawful practices.
15. The objective of the organisation is to make money.

When stating just 15 features of organised crime, it is easy to see the similarities which are found within organised religion.

Unfortunately, religion is often used as a political tool, more than it is used as a means of connecting to the Creator.

Some of the greatest atrocities which have occurred throughout history have occurred as a result of, or in the name of a particular religion.

Searching for the Creator and politics do not mix well. One could even go as far as saying that true religion i.e. connecting with the Creator, and politics are polar opposites.

Connecting with the Creator, means refining one's character traits, broadening one's mind and seeking distance from public authority. Politics on the other hand entails the exact opposite. Politics requires an individual to become egotistical and expedient, closed-minded and in hot pursuit of public authority.

The desire to impose your will onto others is one of the greatest character flaws found within humanity.

Those who are connected to the Creator, run away from honour, while those who are egotistical constantly seek attention and the limelight.

Rabbi Yisrael Meir Kagan of Radin[46] set a wonderful example, and perhaps a moral benchmark that we can aspire to. Rabbi Kagan was so adverse to receiving honour and attention, despite his incredible genius, that he refused to have his picture taken, except for a passport photo.

In rare footage recorded of The First World Congress (Knessia Gedolah) of the World Agudath Israel, which took place in Vienna on, August 15, 1923. Rabbi Kagan can be seen darting off, and deliberately avoiding being caught on film.

Rabbi Kagan captured the sentiment of what it means to be connected to the Creator. The Talmud[47] says "If your Rabbi resembles an angel of God, request Torah knowledge from him".

When searching for the Creator, find for yourself a mentor who is warm-hearted and humble, not an egotistical narcissist. Surround yourself with honest people, and with people who take joy in your success.

[46] Known as the Chofetz Chaim (1838 – 1933)
[47] Moed Katan 17a

11

EMULATING MAN VERSUS EMULATING THE CREATOR

As we discussed earlier; the Creator is such an abstract concept that we can barely comprehend.

The mere concept of prior existence is difficult enough as it is, let alone the concept called "prior pre-existence".

It would seem that only a handful of individuals throughout time, have successfully managed to form a close relationship with the Creator. Perhaps only one in one hundred million people are able to communicate with the Creator in a significant manner.

For the reason of scarcity, it would seem many people are oblivious to the fact, that they in their own personal capacity can form a close and meaningful relationship with the Creator.

For a large majority of people however, finding the Creator, and forming a meaningful relationship, to the point where one is able to circumvent the laws of nature is a complete impossibility.

This is a point of departure:

- Do we accept that our chance of becoming integrated into the supernatural is beyond us, since our chances are, only one in one hundred million?

- Do we work extremely hard, following a prescribed method for achieving spiritual success?

As an analogy, not every human being is capable of becoming a gold medal Olympic athlete. Some individuals will become desponded, and become couch potatoes, knowing their chances are near-impossible, while others will put in huge efforts to train, not because these people think they will become gold medal Olympic athletes, but because they know that something is better than nothing.

In spiritual terms, we often lack confidence in ourselves. We think that prophecy and spiritual awakening is not achievable, and so we look to emulate role-models, instead of becoming role-models ourselves.

These role-models are people who seem to know how to get it right, and in a desperate attempt to accomplish what these role-models have accomplished, we seek to mimic their behaviour in every way possible.

Have you ever asked yourself the question?

1. Could I become greater than Abraham?
2. Could I become greater than Moses?

When one looks at the names above, the first thing one needs to ask is:

1. Did Abraham mimic another human being?
2. Did Moses mimic another human being?

The simple answer to these questions is a stark no!

Yet the above individuals were spiritually successful.

There is only one conclusion to draw, becoming spiritually successful does not require mimicking, or emulating the behaviour of any human being.

In fact, I would argue that quite the opposite is true, mimicking the behaviour of another human being, no matter how great that human being, is one of the biggest obstacles, standing between man and his Creator.

There has never been, nor will there ever be; a spiritually successful person who mimics the behaviour of another human being. Spiritual success is dependent upon individuality.

Spiritual success is dependent upon individuality

The key to spiritual success:

Until one decides that he/she wants to be far greater than Abraham or Moses, he/she will lack the drive needed to achieve any noticeable progress.

It is not the end-goal which is important, but the sheer desire to be the greatest human being to have ever lived.

One who aspires to be close to the Creator, with such passion and desire, will receive "gifts of knowledge" not known to mankind.

The Creator already created an Abraham, and a Moses, the Creator does not need an Abraham Version 2. You were made to be different, and to achieve your own goals.

Unfortunately, a large number of driven individuals have been thoroughly misguided in this area.

While we can most definitely learn, from the great attributes of any great individual, we cannot mimic others.

To learn from another individual, means, to integrate a particular character trait into your own personality, in your own way.

The specialised skill of integrating the observed traits of others requires a highly disciplined mind, and immense mental energy. One who is unable to control his/her thoughts should not bother with this exercise.

Furthermore, one who lacks a pure heart and still bears traces of arrogance should never attempt to mimic the actions of a great individual.

One who lacks a pure heart, or is not willing to spend vast amounts of mental energy on the integration process, will become a shell of a human being, and in most instances the most vile and disgusting human being possible.

Rather be an animal, than a lazy human being mimicking the actions of others.

The integration process:

To integrate a character trait or behaviour, one observes in another requires three elements:

1. One needs to have a complete understanding of one's own character traits both positive and negative. Hence one needs to know themselves thoroughly.
2. One needs to be observant, and awake/aware. A person needs to be so alert that not a single detail of their surroundings is missed.
3. One needs to distill the observed behaviour and transform it into that which is appropriate for one's own character.

The danger:

One, who lacks the aforementioned skills, will undoubtedly misconstrue the observed traits, and turn a positive action into a negative action.

The best advice is to just be yourself, until you have mastered your own thoughts and actions. Try and emulate the actions of the Creator, before you begin the process of emulating the actions of others.

- Emulating the Creator is the definition of greatness, and is the first step in spiritual success.
- Emulating man is dangerous, and reserved for those who have become the master over their own thoughts and actions. Emulating man is a "fine-tuning" for those who have already mastered the art of emulating the Creator.

What is monotheism?

- The word "theism" means belief in a God or Gods, who intervene in the universe.
- The word "mono" comes from the Greek word "monos" meaning singular or one.

Thus monotheism, means believing in a single God who intervenes in the universe.

The character Abraham in the Old Testament, believed to have lived almost 4000 years ago, is often thought of as the father of monotheism.

During the time of Abraham, polytheism or believing in many Gods was the prevailing view, among society. These people, who believed in there being many Gods, are often grouped together and called pagans.

During the lifetime of Abraham, paganism was the popular view and Abraham was a pioneer in convincing people there was only one God.

Abraham was relatively successful, and for many thousands of years there was a well-known saying in the Middle East:

"La illah ila Allah"[48]
"There is no God, but Allah"

However the work of Abraham was not complete, and the majority of the peoples in the Middle East where Abraham lived, still believed in paganism.

[48] The Sira – The Life of Mohamed – Dr. Bill Warner, 2010, CSPI, USA

Abraham was a legend in the Middle East, and almost every person in the region had heard of him. However his views were not accepted by all.

Pagans would not worship a single God, but rather many Gods; the central gathering place for pagan worshippers was in Mecca, Saudi Arabia. For more than two and a half thousand years pagans worshiped a large square rock; known as the "Ka'aba"[49].

The rise of Islam:

More than two and a half thousand years after Abraham, a man arose by the name of Muhammad. This man was not directly related to Abraham in any way, yet he conveyed a message that there is no God but Allah. This was the birth of a new phenomenon called Islam.

Islam is very unique in many ways: Islam is a way of life and not a religion. It is important to note that we are speaking of Islam, and not Muslims, Islam is a doctrine, i.e. what is found in text, while Muslim's refer to people. We are discussing text and not people. Islam has two distinctive elements and two central themes namely:

Elements:

1. There is no God but Allah
2. Muhammad P.B.U.H[50] is the messenger of Allah.

لا إله إلا الله محمد رسول الله

Central themes:

1. Theology - A system of beliefs.
2. Politics - A systematic guide for world domination.

[49] The Ka'aba had a black stone on the top of one of its corners.

[50] P.B.U.H Peace be upon him shall be inferred where omitted.

The prophet Muhammad first taught the Quran in Mecca and over a thirteen year period only amassed approximately 150 followers. The Quran of Mecca is the peaceful Quran which teaches theology. Muhammad asserts that he is the last of the prophets[51], and comes to re-enforce the words of Moses[52].

When Muhammad moved to Medina, he became a warrior and political leader, he taught the Quran of Medina, which primarily deals with politics, and a systematic method of world domination. Muhammad taught virulent hatred for all those who did not follow in his ways.

The Quran of Medina was far more successful, and in Medina Muhammad amassed hundreds of thousands of followers in a very short space of time.

Both the Quran of Medina, which taught religion and the Meccan Quran which taught politics are of equal value. Thus using the concept of dualism, as we mentioned above, both formats of the Quran are accepted.

In reality there are as many as 26 different versions of the Quran, with significant textual variations[53], apart from the 7 well-known reader variations; including Nafi, Ibn Kathir and Abu `Amr al-'Ala' etc.

For our purposes, I would like to discuss just two revolutionary concepts introduced by Muhammad.

1. Muhammad is the messenger of Allah.
2. Political Islam - A systematic guide for world domination.

[51] Surah 33:40
[52] Surah 7: 144
[53] Material for the History of the Text of the Quran, New York, Russell F. Moore, 1952

Muhammad is the messenger of Allah:

Unlike any other faith or political system, Muhammad introduced a very interesting feature into Islam, namely: Muhammad is the perfect human being and the perfect Muslim. Muhammad introduced the world to the concept of emulation.

One cannot talk about Allah without Muhammad - the two are inseparable.

In a study conducted by Dr. Bill Warner, it was found that in the entire corpus of Islamic literature, namely the Sira (the biography of Muhammad), the Hadith (the customs and practices of Muhammad) and the Quran[54].

- There are 91 verses in the Quran which state Muhammad is the perfect Muslim, and that everyone is to copy the actions of Muhammad in the most intricate detail. Those who do not emulate Muhammad in every detail will burn in hellfire.
- The Sira and Hadith make up 86% of the Islamic doctrine, meaning only 14% of Islamic doctrine can be found within the Quran. Thus Islam is 86% about Muhammad and only 14% about Allah.

In essence, Islam is about emulating the prophet Muhammad, and not as much about worshiping Allah.

To classify Islam as monotheistic is somewhat problematic, since the foundation of Islam is centered upon the emulation of a man.

One could state that Islam is:

- Polytheistic - since one needs to worship Allah as Muhammad instructs (thus there are two authority figures)

[54] The Sira, Hadith and Quran make up the trilogy of Islamic belief.

The Quran states[55]

ا فَلَا وَرَبِّكَ لَا يُؤْمِنُونَ حَتَّىٰ يُحَكِّمُوكَ فِيمَا شَجَرَ بَيْنَهُمْ ثُمَّ لَا يَجِدُوا فِي أَنفُسِهِمْ حَرَجًا مِّمَّا قَضَيْتَ وَيُسَلِّمُوا تَسْلِيمًا

"But no, by your Lord, they will not [truly] believe until they make you, [O Muhammad], judge concerning that over which they dispute among themselves and then find within themselves no discomfort from what you have judged and submit in [full, willing] submission."

In Islam, one who does not fully submit to the will of Muhammad is considered an apostate or kafir, and is subject to the death penalty.

Thus in Islam, one has to practice one's life exactly as the prophet Muhammad did, any deviation from emulating Muhammad entirely, is a deviation from Islam.

One, who has not studied the Sira and Hadith extensively, is not a true Muslim. To be a Muslim entails knowing and practicing every detail of one's life as Muhammad did. Even mentally resisting is a form of non-subjugation.

Thus Islam is based almost entirely on emulating the prophet Muhammad, down to the finest detail. A Muslim is compelled to act in exactly the same manner as Muhammad acted, without any hesitation or reluctance, as Muhammad was the perfect Muslim.

Political Islam:

The second and perhaps the most important revolutionary idea Muhammad introduced was that of Political Islam.

The word "Islam" means submission. In particular it means submission to Muhammad and Allah.

[55] Surah 4:64 (4:65 In some editions - Al Nisa about Women)

In Medina, Muhammad was more than a teacher; he was a warrior who controlled armed forces. Using ingenious deception in war, Muhammad used fear to terrorise all those around him into subjugation and submission.

In Medina the concept of jihad was born. "Jihad" which means struggle is a concept found within the Sira, Hadith and Quran.

Jihad takes on two forms:

- An inner struggle, such as overcoming one's temptations.
- An outer struggle, killing the enemies of Islam.

Which struggle is more important in Islam?

The question is sometimes asked, which is more important in Islam, the inner struggle or the outer struggle?

Considering the texts, the inner struggle only accounts for 2% of the content, whereas 98% of the content deals with the outer struggle[56].

Thus 98% of jihad is focused on killing the enemies of Islam, and killing they did; Muhammad waged a war on average every six weeks, for the last nine years of his life.

Islam was spread throughout the world, using jihad or "Political Islam", very successfully.

Political Islam has the sole objective, of making the entire planet governed by Sharia law (Islamic law).

There is absolutely no aspect of conduct found within civilization that is not covered and governed by Sharia Law.

Unlike Christianity which does not have laws regulating daily practices, Islam has a strict set of laws which are applied to daily living:

[56] According to the statistical study of Dr. Bill Warner

- From drinking a glass of water, to going to the bathroom.
- From marriage to divorce.
- From birth to death.

In Islam there is a law for everything; Islam is a complete guide to controlling a civilization - no action falls outside of the scope of Islam, if Mohammad did it, then so must every Muslim.

Three levels of jihad:

Although killing the enemies of Islam is of utmost importance in seeking world domination, it is not always possible to kill non-Muslims. Therefore although jihad is the primary objective[57], in some countries and during some periods in history, jihad had to be conducted in a clever manner.

As the prophet Muhammad said[58]:

"الحرب خُدعة"وعنه وعن جابر، رضي الله عنهما أن النبي صلى الله عليه وسلم قال:

War is deception

In order to conduct the war against the enemies of Islam, deception is needed in order for the enemy not to know the strategy. This deception is known as **"Taqiyya".**

"Taqiyya" or deception in jihad was used successfully during:

- The defeat of the Jews in Arabia in the late 600's CE.
- The defeat of the Europeans from the year 732 CE.
- The Crusades between the years 1095-1291 CE, Where Islam defeated Christianity.
- In 1453 where the Ottoman Turks defeated the Byzantine Empire.

[57] Surah 2:25

[58] Book 12, Hadith 68, Al-Bukhari and Muslim (Mash'hur and Sahi)

Level one jihad:

When the enemies of Islam are the dominant force within a particular region, for example in a country where the majority of citizens are non-Muslim, it would be impractical to kill all non-Muslims.

In Islam it is forbidden to befriend a non-Muslim[59], thus Islam teaches that one should practice "Taqiyya" (deception), by outwardly acting friendly but hating the enemy in your heart.

In these circumstances the fight of jihad, is to receive special privileges or benefits for Islam, within such a country or region. By fighting for special privileges, one is elevating Islam.

Level two jihad:

When Islam is more powerful within a particular region, for example in a country that allows free speech, or if the country sees all of its citizens as equals, regardless of their religion - jihad can move up a notch, by openly criticising all non-Muslims, and waging enticement and provocation towards all the enemies of Islam.

Level two jihad will be called terrorism by the enemies of Islam, or freedom fighting by those adhering to Islam.

In these circumstances the fight of jihad, is to terrorise and frighten all those whom are considered the enemy of Islam, thus striking fear into the hearts of all non-believers.

Level three jihad:

When Islam is in the majority, or is the dominant culture within a particular region or country, then jihad can take place in its ultimate form.

The ultimate form of jihad is to kill all non-believers, or at the very least to subjugate other people into "Dhimmi" (second class) status.

[59] Surah 3:28

In these circumstances the fight of jihad, is to uphold Sharia law as the law of the land, and to bolster Islam, into conquering new territories.

Thus Islam clearly lays out a step-by-step approach to world domination. There is no circumstance in which the objectives of Islam cannot be furthered.

Who is an enemy of Islam?

In Islam there are two categories:

1. Muslims - those who practice Islam.
2. Non-Muslims - those who reject Islam.

Any person who rejects Islam for whatever reason or even one who does not fully and wholeheartedly submit to the will of Allah and Muhammad is termed a "kafir" (non-believer).

Every kafir is any enemy of Islam.

The trilogy of Islam devotes a large portion of its text to; describing who a kafir is and what exactly should be done to the kafir.

- Quran - 64% is about kafirs.
- Sira - 81% is about kafirs.
- Hadith - 37% about kafirs.

Thus 60% of all Islamic text is devoted to the treatment of the kafir, whilst only 40% deals with the conduct purely for Muslim use[60].

[60] Dr. Bill Warner

Who is a kafir?

The Christians and the Jews are considered kafirs in Islamic text.

Let us briefly look at some of the verses in the Quran.

"They indeed have disbelieved who say: Lo! Allah is the Messiah, son of Mary. Say: Who then can do aught against Allah, if He had willed to destroy the Messiah son of Mary, and his mother and everyone on earth?"[61]

"The foolish ones will say, "What makes them turn from the kiblah [the direction they faced during Islamic prayer]?" Say: Both the east and the west belong to Allah. He will guide whom He likes to the right path. We have made you [Muslims] the best of nations so that you can be witnesses over the world and so that the messenger may be a witness for you. We appointed the former kiblah towards Jerusalem and now Mecca."[62]

"To those of you [Jews and Christians] to whom the Scriptures were given: Believe in what We have sent down confirming the Scriptures you already possess before we destroy your faces and twist your heads around backwards, or curse you as we did those [the Jews] who broke the Sabbath for Allah's commandments will be carried out."[63]

•

[61] Surah 5:16
[62] Surah 2:141
[63] Surah 4:46

Furthermore:

Anyone from any other religion is considered a kafir.

"And whoso seek as religion other than the Surrender (to Allah) it will not be accepted from him, and he will be a loser in the Hereafter."[64]

The apostate i.e. one who left Islam: is also considered a kafir.

"They swear by Allah that they said nothing wrong, yet they spoke blasphemy, and some Muslims became Kafirs…"[65]

The kafir:

- "Seize them and slay them where ever you find them." [66]
- "For the kafirs are open enemies to you"[67]
- "For the kafirs, Allah has prepared a humiliating punishment."[68]

In conclusion:

Emulating a man, often leads to unfound hatred of the human species.

Although the emulation of man; can bring about world domination through fear and submission, this domination usually leads to the death of millions.

Some believe the fall of the Roman Empire, was due to the fact that the Romans adopted Christianity, which for the most part shuns warfare, and they thus lost their military prowess.

However the opposite extreme, of killing everyone other than your own group, seems just as counterproductive.

[64] Surah 3:84
[65] Surah 9:73
[66] Surah 4:88
[67] Surah 4:100
[68] Surah 4:101

As for Islam, the duties of a Muslim are primarily to worship Allah and fight for the sake of Allah's greatness.

Being a zealot has its place in the world, perhaps Mohammad saw that the fastest way to spread fear and awe of the Creator was through being a zealot.

After all, the Creator is great, and must be acknowledged. The only problem with using fear as a persuasive method is that although it speaks to man's primary instincts, and delivers fast results, once the fear is removed people will return to their natural state.

Thus the only way to impose this fear is to tightly hold subjects within its grip, and dispose of any subjects who resist this grip.

Using fear alone may also have the opposite effect and cause people to move further away since people are more attracted to love.

Therefore a Muslim may have a difficult task ahead of him/her since he/she must emulate the prophet of Islam, and has little room to give expression to their own uniqueness.

A Muslim may have a difficult task ahead of him/her since he/she must emulate the prophet of Islam, and has little room to give expression to their own uniqueness.

Christians may also have a difficult task ahead of them, since Christianity also involves the emulation of a man, albeit to a lesser degree.

One of the largest religions in the world today is Christianity, and one of the key figures in Christianity is a character named Jesus.

In this section I would like to expand on the following concepts, as they pertain to one whom is in search of the Creator.

1. Who was Jesus?
2. When did Jesus live?
3. Did Jesus start the religion known today as Christianity?
4. What religion did Jesus follow?

To answer these questions, we will need to explore the history of this subject in greater detail, giving special attention to the rise and fall of the Roman Empire, as well as the setting and culture found in Mesopotamia many years ago.

In short the answers to the above questions are as follows:

1. Jesus was a rabbi in Mesopotamia.
2. Jesus lived sometime in the period 30 BCE.
3. No, Jesus did not start Christianity. Christianity was started by the Romans, hence the term Roman-Catholic.
4. Jesus was Jewish, and followed the religion of Judaism.

We will now go deeper into this subject, to explore how we can come to the answers given above.

Do you believe in Jesus?

Very often a Christian is asked the question: "Do you believe in Jesus?" For me I am less interested in the answer, as I am in the question.

What in the world does it mean to believe in Jesus? Some offer the following as explanations of this question.

A. Do you believe that Jesus existed?
B. Do you believe that Jesus was not a human being?
C. Do you believe that Jesus is the son of God?
D. Do you believe that Jesus died for our sins?

If we go with the option above, do you believe that Jesus existed?

Most scholars do agree that although the name Jesus was very common in Mesopotamia in the years 100 BCE to 100 CE, there was in fact one Jesus who was unique in the sense that he had some sort of following of people, and was somewhat influential. Hence the character found in the New Testament known as Jesus of Nazareth, did in fact exist.

One of the external sources which are cited as evidence for the existence of the character known as Jesus is the Babylonian Talmud[69], compiled in Babylon, Mesopotamia in the year 300 CE (approximately). We will elaborate on the Talmud and the various versions in the section entitled "The Talmud".

However, there are scholars such as Earl Doherty[70], who contend that Jesus did not exist as a historical figure. There are also scholars such as Randel Helms[71] who asserts that the gospels are fictional works, creating a fictional character named "Jesus of Nazareth".

[69] Sanhedrin 43 (Not found in classic Vilna edition) and Gittin 57a (Reference to Bilam in Vilna edition)
[70] Author of the Jesus puzzle
[71] Author of "Gospel Fictions"

The philosopher Stephen Law[72] has written a very eloquent scholarly article, which asserts that there is not enough evidence to prove beyond a reasonable doubt that the character in the New Testament named Jesus actually existed, nor do we have good independent evidence, to corroborate much of what is said in the New Testament, and thus one should remain skeptical about his existence.

However based on the majority of scholars, one can assume that Jesus did in fact exist. If believing in Jesus, simply means believing that there was a person named Jesus, then the majority of rational and scholarly individuals would attest to the fact that they do believe that there was a person named Jesus.

If we go with the option "do you believe that Jesus was not a human being?"

As will be discussed below, the Visigoths[73], the Goths from the west believed Jesus was not a human being or mere mortal. The art work from that period depicts Jesus with a halo above his head, indicating his angel-like status.

On the other hand the Ostrogoths[74], the Goths from the east believed Jesus was a normal human being. His refined character traits and other personal attributes made him an exceptional human being, but a human being nonetheless. Artwork from the Ostrogoth collection depicts Jesus as a human being, with a crown of thorns, rather than a halo on his head.

Thus the question of whether or not Jesus was a human being has two distinctive schools of thought.

---

[72] Faith and Philosophy, Volume 28, Issue 2, April 2011, Stephen Law, Pages 129-151, Evidence, Miracles, and the Existence of Jesus

[73] Western branches of the nomadic tribes of Germanic peoples referred to collectively as the Goths. Approximately from the year 300 CE

[74] Goths from the Black Sea to the Baltic, approximately from the year 300 CE

If we go with the option "do you believe that Jesus is the son of God?"

The answer to this question seems somewhat puzzling. First of all can the Creator even have a son? If the Creator is in essence a being of prior pre-existence, and beyond the spiritual realm, as discussed earlier, then such a being cannot by definition have any physical descendants. Hence, the Creator cannot have any human offspring, as the Creator is not human. Thus the Creator can bear no children, be it son or daughter.

Hence the Creator has no literal son.

Even if the Creator were to miraculously cause a woman to conceive, the resulting offspring would have questionable origin, namely is this child a human being or not? This concept, which was dealt with in option "B" above, takes us back and one would need to investigate the format of conception, of Jesus's mother.

The belief that Jesus is the son of the Creator is a contradiction in terms; either the Creator is a human being, capable of fathering children, or the Creator is a being of prior pre-existence and both Jesus and his mother are the equivalent of the Creator.

If there are two other beings which are equivalent to the Creator, then the Creator is not one and unique. This belief would therefore be polytheistic in nature, and a huge divergence away from monotheism.

For those who postulate that Jesus was the son of God, the explanation given is that the Creator incarnated as a human being, and impregnated the mother of Jesus in the normal fashion.

Thus, it could be said that Jesus had a natural mother who was a human being, and a father whom was an incarnate human being at the time of conception.

Thus Jesus had two biological parents who were human beings, and it would be more accurate to say Jesus is the son of the human being incarnated by the Creator.

"Extraordinary claims require extraordinary evidence"[75]

Apart from the fact that laying such extraordinary claims, that the Creator incarnated himself into the form of a human being, is an exceptionally grand assertion, requiring extraordinary evidence to support such a claim, there is another problem with this belief.

Another more pressing issue is the fact that there is no precedent or source for this ever occurring elsewhere.

This in fact would be the grandest miracle to occur in the history of the universe. Nowhere else in biblical literature, do we find that the Creator takes on the form of a human being, apart from this one particular event, involving a person named Jesus.

Furthermore, the need to create a "son" figure seems extraneous and somewhat peculiar. I have not found just cause, to complicate matters with regards to the existence and workings of the Creator, as well as the functioning of the universe.

- What purpose does the "son" have?
- Why was this "son" not created as "Adam"?
- Why was this "son" not made together with the construction of the universe?
- In essence why would the Creator, suddenly choose to have a child in the year 30 BCE?

Having a firm belief in the Creator, and the creation of the universe, does not require the belief in an "ancestry" of the Creator.

[75] Carl Sagan

If Jesus himself had a son, which he may have:

- Would this child be considered the grandson of the Creator?
- Would the grandson and future descendants, play any important role?
- Is the family tree of Jesus intact until this day?
- Do the descendants of Jesus have any supernatural powers?

I have found that introducing a "son" into the mix;

- At best needlessly complicates matters of theology and monotheism.
- At worst, is full-fledged polytheism, almost indistinguishable from other pagan religions.

If we go with the option "do you believe that Jesus died for our sins?"

The concept of righteous individuals, taking upon themselves, either willingly or unwillingly, pain and suffering, on behalf of others, is not a foreign concept in many theologies.

For example the Talmud cites[76] the sage Rava, who would request sicknesses upon himself in order to atone for the sins of his generation.

The Talmud states: "Whoever cries over the loss of a good man, the Creator counts his tears, and places them in his treasury."[77]

The Talmud also states: Who ever cries over the death of a good man, the Creator forgives him for all his sins."[78]

[76] Makkos 11a
[77] Shabbos 105b
[78] Ibid

We find numerous individuals, who were martyred, in Jewish history. One of the most famous is that of the "Ten Martyrs" sages in the period 300 CE (approximately)[79].

Who were brutally murdered by the Romans, as atonement for the sins of several generations of Jewish people.[80] Thus the concept of one man being punished for the sins of others is not a foreign concept.

What is foreign however, is the concept of retroactivity. I.e. paying in advance for sins, which have yet to be committed.

In all other known examples, of where an individual martyr; who was either killed, or suffered as atonement for the sins of his/her generation - the individual was "paying" for sins which had already been committed in the past.

These individuals died for sins which were already committed in the past. Never do we have an example, apart from Jesus, of an individual being martyred as atonement for sins of future generations, which have yet to have been committed.

The death of Jesus can be viewed as a credit facility. It offers all sinners past, present and future, a way to absolve themselves from sin, by placing their misdeeds on Jesus's "tab". The account of all wrong-doing will be settled by Jesus.

This concept is akin to going to a restaurant, and ordering all you can eat, and then paying for the bill using someone else's credit card.

Having another individual bear the responsibility for your actions seems like a way to avoid responsibility.

Taking the stance, that the death of one individual many years ago; somehow absolves future generations from punishment, comes across as a way to deflect responsibility, for an individual in the present.

[79] Commonly known as the "Asara Harugay Malchus"

It seems irrational and perhaps irresponsible, to act however which way you please, and then expect someone else, to take the fall, for your actions.

Surely a rational and responsible individual would assume responsibility for their own actions, and then face the consequences of those actions?

If one does not assume responsibility for the bad actions and can therefore avoid any form of punishment, why then would one receive any reward for good deeds?

Logically speaking; when one has no consequences for their actions, one severs the actor from the actions, and the ensuing consequences. Thus with no attachment to the action, the actor is removed from the equation all together.

This would be the ultimate form of "having your cake and eating it". This belief system assumes that, you are not punished for your bad deeds, but you are rewarded for your good deeds. It does sound appealing, but is logically flawed.

As a case in point; would we ever allow the perpetrator of a crime, say a murderer or a rapist, to walk off scot-free, using the defense that Jesus has already paid for the crime in advance?

If Jesus did in fact die for our sins, then why bother trying to be a good person? For no matter what you do, you are never personally responsible for your own actions.

In conclusion, option "D" seems to be the most irrational, self-serving and irresponsible belief to have.

[80] Talmud Sanhedrin 48b, Avoda Zara 17b and Jewish Liturgy (Tisha B'Av and Yom Kippur)

Thus, all we can say with a sense of rationality is that Jesus most likely existed. What that means in practical terms would appear to be inconsequential.

Many of the popular beliefs held about Jesus, come from the gospels, as well as a distortion of facts. We will briefly look at some of the gospels in reference, and understand their meaning in context.

In order to gain a better understanding of the character known as Jesus, we will need to examine the rise and fall of the Roman Empire, and the role which the Romans took in the formation of the religion known as Christianity.

The rise and fall of the Roman Empire:

"That which was, will be, and that which occurred, will occur,
And there is nothing new under the sun"[81]

In the book of Ecclesiastes, King Solomon points out the nature of history. If we want to understand the present, and even predict the future, all we need to do, is to examine the past.

History repeats itself; the names and locations may change with time, yet the underlying concepts of what drives humanity are a constant with no variation.

An individual, who has a thorough knowledge of history, from all perspectives[82], will have enormous insight into current day events, and will be acutely aware of the events, which lay waiting in the future.

[81] Ecclesiastes 1:9

[82] Not just the victors, but the losers of battles etc.

The closest thing we have to prophets today, are our historians.

Why is the Roman Empire so important?

There were a number of great empires which existed in history, some examples of which include:

1. The Chinese Empire
2. The Egyptian Empire
3. The Empire of the Hans
4. The Etruscan Empire
5. The Greek Empire
6. The Mongolian Empire
7. The Persian Empire

Each and every empire, in history had its unique qualities, culture, accomplishments and failures. Each had its lessons to teach to humanity.

Our everyday lives are still influenced by the Roman Empire

The study of every empire, and in fact any historical event, period and even unique individuals from a given era, such as Alexandra the Great, Napoleon or Adolf Hitler; yields insights into the nature of human beings, and expands the mind of all those who study them.

The Roman Empire, is particularly unique however, and worthy of our attention. Apart from the fact that our everyday lives are still influenced by the Roman Empire, and Roman culture[83], what we would call "Western culture", the Roman Empire was one of the longest-lasting empires ever to have existed. Its cultural value system changed the world, like no other empire before it.

[83] Our legal system is based on Roman law

As far as Western culture goes, Rome gave birth to some of the novel concepts, we take for granted today. Words such as republic, senate and dictator did not exist before the Romans introduced them, and yet today these words are alive and still have meaning.

So much can be learned from the almost 1000 year period, that a study of the Roman Empire is akin to the greatest longitudinal study, or social experiment ever conducted.

Having a "snap-shot" of humanity spanning 1000 years, gives us an opportunity to peek into the inner workings of human nature, and allows us to glean insights into the human condition in a way that can't be done otherwise.

This snapshot is like an X-ray of the human condition. Not enough can be said about the importance of studying history.

Since the Roman Empire spanned a period of almost 1000 years, we will only briefly mention some of the highlights, as they pertain to one who is in search of the Creator.

Much of what we know about the Roman Empire comes from the historians who lived in the age of antiquity.

We will primarily make use of two historians, for our purposes:

- Plutarch (46 -120 CE): Plutarch was a Greek man who later became a Roman citizen. One of his famous works entitled "Parallel Lives", gives a detailed biography of many of the Roman leaders, and sheds light on many of the historical events of that time.
- Livy (64 BC - 17 CE) Livy lived before Plutarch, and his work entitled "Ab Urbe Condita Libri" Livy describes the founding of the Roman Empire, as well as biographic details on Rome's many leaders.

The founding of Rome: (The era of monarchy)

Around the year 800 BC, Rome was simply a village. Much of the area was swamp land and the geographical location was home to many various tribes of varying origins.

- From the period 753 BC - 509 BC, Rome was ruled by a monarch.
- Mythical legend states, that around the year 800 BC, two twin boys were born[84] and abandoned by their parents in the woods. The names of these two boys were Romulus and Remus. Both Romulus and Remus were brought up by a feral wolf in the forest, and these boys are thought to have been the sons of the gods.
- In a heated argument Romulus, killed his brother Remus, and became the first King of Rome, naming the city after himself and the goddess Roma.
- Rome had a series of kings, who came from the ruling elite class as follows[85]:
    1. Romulus (753-717 BC)
    2. Numa (717 - 673 BC) - known as the law giver.
    3. Tullus Hostilius (672 - 641 BC)
    4. Ancus Marcius (639 - 616 BC)
    5. Tarquinius Priscus (616 - 579 BC)
    6. Servius Tullius (579 -534 BC)
    7. Tarquinius Superbus (534 - 510 BC)

- During this early period there was great hostility between Romans and Etruscans. The Etruscans were more technologically advanced, and the kings were predominantly Etruscans. Romans disliked the Etruscans due to their lack of moral values, which included sexual promiscuity in public.

[84] A similar rendition of the Biblical story of Kain and Able, as well as Jacob and Esau

[85] Thomas Robert Shannon Broughton, The Magistrates of the Roman Republic, vol. I (Philological Monograph No. 15), American Philological Association, New York (1951)

- After a great battle the Romans beat their Etruscan neighbours, and installed Sextus Tarquinius, the son of Tarquinius Superbus, as the Roman ruler.
- During the reign of kings, only the noble elite had knowledge of the laws, and controlled the masses with an "iron fist". The common folk had no say in state affairs and lived in a state of fear and intimidation from their wealthier rulers.
- In the year 509 BC, a brand new system was developed within the governance of Rome, and Rome became a republic.

The Republic of Rome:

From the year 509 BC to the year 49 CE, Rome was classified as a republic. The concept of a republic comes from the Latin words "Res Publica", meaning that officials are elected by the people.

- The letters S.P.Q.R., became the motto for the newly formed republic. These letters stood for "The Senate and the people of Rome".
- One of the main goals of the republic was to bring balance to Roman civilisation. The commoners wanted a voice in deciding who should lead them and how they should be treated.
- In the republic there were two classes of individuals.
    A. The Patricians - the wealthy aristocrats
    B. The Plebeians - the poor peasants[86]
- Under the old monarch system of Rome, only the elite were privy to the laws, which they used to oppress the poor. In the new Republic of Rome, the Plebeians forced the laws to be made public, in order for every Roman citizen to take full advantage of the law.

[86] Later a third class developed called Equites, who were comprised of Plebeians wealthy enough to purchase a horse and go into battle.

- The system of government comprised of a Senate, Consuls and Magistrates / Tribunes. The senate was comprised mainly of the wealthy elite who would guide the consuls on what laws to create or revoke.
- The consuls were like modern-day presidents. They were seen as the rulers of Rome.
- Consuls came in sets of two[87], similar to a president and a vice president. However each consul was an equal president, and as such Rome was ruled by a dual president. Each consul had the right to veto, a ruling passed by his counterpart consul. There was a balance or cross checks in place, to ensure that no one consul would pass laws solely for his own benefit, but rather for the benefit of Rome.
- Consuls had a term limit of one year, after which that individual could not be elected again for another ten years.
- The Plebeians were given representation in the senate, and were given special veto powers. The Plebeian representative could revoke any passed law which was deemed not to be in the best interests of the Plebeian community. Thus in the new Republic the Plebeians were given quite a large amount of power, which helped to restore the economic inequality within society.
- Another feature of the Republic was the allowance of a dictator. A dictator was an individual who had powers exceeding all other members of government, and who ruled entirely on his own. A dictator was installed in times of emergency[88], due to a foreign or domestic threat. A dictator had a term limit of six months after which the government would revert back to its normal functioning.
- When Rome was a republic it enjoyed great success. When the Romans expanded their empire they would often incorporate, values and cultures of the newly conquered territories.

[87] In later periods sets of 4 and 6 individuals

The rise of the Roman Republic:

Rome reached its apex, in terms of territory-holding and dominion, somewhere in the period between 100 - 200 CE.

Greater than the territory held by Alexander the Great, the Roman Empire was perhaps the first civilisation to conquer the entire known world.

At its height, Rome stretched from London to Baghdad, controlled nearly every shipping port, had a first class professional army, and boasted many grand mega-structures, made of concrete, superior to the quality found today.

Rome had a complex system of aqueducts, providing running water to every home, as well as highly detailed sewerage systems.

Rome had magnificent super highways and bridges, joining almost every region in its vast empire. It would be possible for an individual to cross nearly 2.2 million square miles (5.7 million square kilometres) using a single passport and a single currency.

Despite this great prosperity however, there were "cracks" in the system. The socio-economic disparity was immense, with the ultra-wealthy enjoying every delicacy possible, and the peasants living a harsh and brutal existence.

Even though the republic gave some power to the lower classes, not all men were born equal. Corruption was rife in Rome, and in the year 113 BC a man by the name of Papirius Carbo bought the position of consul. Thus the democracy of elected officials was not quite all it was intended to be.

[88] Similar to the term "State of Emergency"

Corruption:

Carbo was of noble descent, and was extraordinarily wealthy. The culture of the elite ruling over the "plebs" still prevailed. Apart from wealth, honour was earned in Rome by showing military prowess.

Although Carbo bought one of the highest positions in the Roman government, he had absolutely no military experience. He thus had to "prove" himself to the Roman public.

Carbo led several thousand men to war, in the hope of conquering new territories, to expand the Roman Empire, and thus winning the favour of the populace. Due to Carbo's lack of military experience however, as many as eighty thousand Roman soldiers were killed, and Carbo returned back home to Rome where he committed suicide in disgrace.

Bending the rules:

According to Roman law, a consul could only rule for a period of one year, after which he could not be re-elected for a period of ten years.

In the year 104 BC however, a man by the name of Marius was elected as consul. Marius allowed Plebeians to join the Roman army, to replace the casualties caused by Carbo.

Due to his continuous victories in battles, and his overwhelming popularity among both the Roman soldiers as well as the general public, Marius was re-elected as consul in the year 103 BC, again in the year 102 BC, and yet again in the years 101 and 100 BC. Marius ruled for five consecutive years, which was technically illegal, thus the laws of Rome became somewhat flexible, to suit the needs of the popular opinion.

Forced slavery:

When the Romans conquered new territories, they would often take the inhabitants of the newly acquired land, and sell them as slaves.

For some, a worse fate was in store. The Romans would often take male prisoners, and force them to become gladiators.

The term gladiator conjures up images of strong warriors, but in truth it had a far more sinister meaning.

Every year the Romans would hold a "sporting" event, where spectators were entertained by watching the gruesome death of slaves.

In this blood sport, wild animals such as starving lions were set upon helpless victims, and the spectators watched the victims being mauled to death.

One of the highlights of this event was the gladiator fight. The gladiator, who was a slave partially trained in military combat, was paired up against a well-trained Roman soldier for a hand-to-hand fight.

The gladiator had no armour, and no weapons, while the Roman soldier would be fully armoured and fully armed.

The crowd would often pick the weapon, they wanted the gladiator to face. More often than not the gladiator would be beaten to death, by the Roman soldier, and suffer a slow and agonising death, all for the amusement of the crowd.

In the year 73 BC, two well-known gladiators decided to launch a rebellion against the Romans, and their cruel and humiliating practices.

These two men were: Spartacus and Crixus. A year later, in the year 72 BC, Spartacus and Crixus had a disagreement and parted ways.

The Romans eventually found Crixus, and killed him in a surprise attack. However Spartacus, who was in hiding, continued to wreak havoc, and humiliate the Romans.

The following year in 71 BC, Crassus, a well-respected Roman military commander, decided to find and defeat Spartacus once and for all, for the sake of Rome, and bringing an end to the humiliation of the Roman Empire.

However, his true motivation behind finding Spartacus was to achieve further fame and glory for himself, as well as to advance his own military career.

Unfortunately for Crassus, at the same time he began his operation to defeat Spartacus; Pompey who was an even greater general than Crassus, returned from Spain, after achieving a huge military victory there, Pompey, not Crassus was eventually given the credit for killing Spartacus.

Although Crassus mounted the majority of the war, Pompey came in towards the end, and took credit for defeating Spartacus[89].

In order to create a deterrent for other would-be rebels; Pompey crucified Spartacus, along with 6000 other men, and hung their crucified bodies along the road leading to Rome, a distance of 125 miles (202 km).

Plutarch notes, that many of the men took days to die, and the streets of Rome, bore a stench of rotting corpses.

[89] Pompey had a reputation for coming in just prior to victory, and then taking full credit for the success.

This was the cruel and gruesome side of the Roman Empire, which is sometimes forgotten.

Julius Caesar and the end of the Roman Republic:

By the year 65 BC, riots and political upheaval, were the norm in Rome; social inequality had reached its tipping point.

Julius Caesar was a great people's person, and a charismatic public speaker. He was sent to Hispania to do his military training; there he showed great potential, and military skill.

Although Caesar came from the aristocracy of Rome, he saw himself as someone who could relate to the common folk of Rome. Caesar even raised his illegitimate son Marcus Brutus into the political fold of Rome.

Caesar was heavily indebted however, and was in desperate need of money. Caesar set his eyes on the provinces of Gaul, knowing that if he were to reign over those provinces, it would bring an end to his financial woes.

Caesar used his powers, of influence and persuasion, to form an alliance with Crassus the wealthiest man in Rome, and Pompey the most powerful military commander.

With two great backers at his side, Caesar quickly ascended to recognised power within the Roman senate.

Pompey and Crassus convinced the Roman senate that Caesar should be given the provinces of Gaul. The senate complied, and they not only gave Caesar the Southern provinces of Gaul, but also allowed him to expand and take the Northern provinces of Gaul.

Caesar grabbed this opportunity, and by the year 58 BC, was on a rampage to conquer new lands. His army was richly rewarded with spoils, and became very loyal to Caesar, killing hundreds of thousands in their wake.

Just four years later, in 54 BC, Caesar crossed over into Britannia, something none of his predecessors had done before. In Britannia he amassed even more wealth, and greater military command.

Back in Rome, the elite became increasingly concerned that Caesar would break ranks, and become a representative of the commoners. The elite wanted to hold onto power and were greatly disturbed by the changes, being brought about by Caesar, and his growing support from the military as well as his popularity with the people.

By this time, Rome was in political turmoil. There were open skirmishes on the streets, with some supporting change, and others supporting the status quo. During this period of social unrest, the senate building was burnt down.

In the camps of Caesar, the battles continued. A character by the name of Mark Anthony became a close subordinate of Caesar.

After the death of Pompey's wife and child, being the daughter of Caesar and his grandchild respectively, Pompey was overcome with grief and broke ties with Caesar. Furthermore, Pompey was persuaded by the senate to join the conservative elite, and cut all formal connections with Caesar.

By the year 52 BC, Caesar crossed over into the Germanic lands, expanding the empire further than had been done by any of his predecessors, eclipsing the great conqueror Pompey himself.

Caesar wished to return to Rome as a hero; however he was more of a threat, than a hero figure to most. Jealousy made Caesar an enemy, in the eyes of many.

In the year 49 BC, Pompey fled to Greece, a place where he could muster up more support. Caesar chased Pompey to Greece, and a great civil war broke out between Pompey's army and Caesar's army the following year.

Caesar defeated Pompey, but Pompey escaped to Egypt, where he was eventually killed. The severed head of Pompey was then brought back to Caesar.

In the year 46 BC, Rome was totally controlled by Caesar, and two years later in the year 44 BC, Caesar declared himself "King of Rome".

On the 15th of March of that same year, Caesar was assassinated by a group of 40 men led by his own son, Brutus. Caesar was stabbed multiple times and left for dead.

The death of Julius Caesar; did not bring about any stability in Rome, in fact quite the opposite happened. From this time onwards a new period began in a Rome - the period of Emperors had begun.

The Emperor of Rome:

After the death of Julius Caesar, Rome entered the historical period lasting almost 200 hundred years, sometimes referred to as Pax Romana (Roman Peace), Rome expanded its control, conquered new territories and set up a new system of governance known as the Roman Principate.

Gaius Octavius was named in Caesar's will as his adopted son and sole heir. Octavius thus inherited a vast fortune from his great uncle, and was thrust into a position of power.

Gaius Octavius changed his name to "Imperātor Caesar Dīvī Fīlius Augustus" - a Latin term meaning "Commander Caesar, son of God[90]".

Octavius more commonly known as Augustus was the first Emperor of Rome. Augustus first formed a Triumvirate (a three-way partnership of power). Augustus's partnership was with Mark Anthony and Marcus Lepidus, both of who were close allies of Julius Caesar.

[90] A term which would be used to describe Jesus

At first, Octavius/ Augustus ruled the Western provinces, Antony ruled the Eastern provinces, and Lepidus ruled Africa. However, internal strife broke down this partnership, leaving Augustus as the complete ruler of the entire Roman Empire.

Augustus set up a system of governance, which is still widely used to the present day. This includes calling himself "The first citizen"[91] as well as establishing formal courts, civil policing, fire brigades and special armed forces known as the Praetorian Guard.

During the lifetime of Augustus, the Roman Empire expanded into Germania, Dalmatia, Pannonia, Noricum, as well as parts of Africa. The mission of the Roman Emperor; was not just conquering new lands, but also about expanding the Roman culture.

The Romans believed their culture was far superior to that of any other, and it was their duty to share this culture, with the uncultured barbarians that surrounded them. We see this concept many centuries later, with British colonialism, where the goal was also about educating the natives on, the culture of the Empire.

As to be expected, being forced to adopt Roman culture was incredibly unpleasant for many people. Many whole tribes committed suicide rather than having to abandon their centuries-old culture and preferred way of life.

In some regions, the natives fought the Romans passionately to retain their own independence; often resulting in massive causalities on both sides.

Some peoples capitulated to Roman rule, usually by way of the Roman governor of that territory, paying money to the existing authority of that particular group of people.

[91] Airforce one is a prime example

Keeping the existing power structure of a conquered nation in place, is a good way to ensure stability of the region: the common folk still see familiar faces as their rulers, without knowing their rulers are subservient to a foreign authority. Adolf Hitler used this technique successfully when he invaded France.

One needs to bear in mind, that conquering a new land takes more than winning a battle. One needs to have a follow-up plan, of how to ensure stability in the newly conquered region.

One of the tactics used by the Romans, was that of the governor or "satellite ruler". The governor of a newly acquired territory would receive his command directly from Rome, and then implement the laws and rulings in the land he governed.

There were many emperors of Rome, each with a wholesome story. For our purposes we will not delve further into the Roman Empire's history as such, other than to note two important historical events:

1. The destruction of the Second Temple in Jerusalem in the year 70 CE.
2. The division and eventual collapse of the Roman Empire, starting in the year 260 CE.

Further reading is advised, in order to gain a more comprehensive understanding of this topic. For our purposes, we are skimming just the "tip of the iceberg", to glean some perspective, and place this topic in context.

Jerusalem and the Second Temple:

The Talmud[92] tells us that 180 years prior to the destruction of the Second Temple, the political climate in Jerusalem began to change.

---

[92] Avoda Zara 7b

This would place us in the year 110 BC[93], during the period where Rome was a republic, and perhaps ruled by Marius.

The Talmud elaborates on that time period, and further states, that for a period of 28 years (from 110 - 82 BC) the Romans and the Jews had a diplomatic and cordial relationship with one another. Later the relationship began to sour, perhaps under the ruler Lucius Cornelius Cinna.

As we stated earlier, one of the primary goals of Roman expansion was to "re-educate" the uncivilised people, and to give the "backward" nations the "gift" of Roman culture.

Furthermore, in the overwhelming majority of territories conquered by the Romans, there existed a culture of its own, among the peoples of that region.

Each region had its own unique culture, including way of dress, code of conduct, socially accepted norms, as well as a belief system[94].

Jerusalem was no different, and it was home to a sect of people known as the Jews. The Jews had long been worshipping in their Temple, which was rebuilt in the year 516 BC.

By the year 82 BC, the Jews had a long-established culture centered on temple service, for more than 400 years, based on their-own religion of Judaism which was already over 1500 years old by that time.

As was the case for all territories governed by Roman rule, a satellite ruler / governor was put in place to ensure the stability of the region, as well as compliance to Roman law.

[93] The exact calendar year is not known due to the discrepancies in the Julian calendar.

[94] Usually some form of paganism

Jerusalem was a thriving metropolis, and had been a key city for many centuries. When the Roman / Jewish relationship began to sour in the year 82 BC, a problem emerged.

At first the Roman laws passed against the Jewish people were just burdensome. Over time however; these laws became more and more repressive in nature, until the point of ultimate hostility with brute force and public executions.

As a part of Roman culture, the wealthiest among people were considered the best and therefore fit to rule. However, Jewish culture was in stark contrast to that system. Jewish culture maintained that the most righteous individuals were best fit to rule, regardless of their financial standing. Furthermore, certain temple services could only be conducted by specific family lines. For example, only a Kohen[95] could serve in the inner sanctum of the temple, and only a Levite could perform auxiliary services.

However, when the Romans came to Jerusalem, they re-organised the Jewish population; in such a way that positions of power, status and authority were given to the wealthiest, as was the custom of Rome.

The old dictum: "When in Rome, do as the Romans do" was scaled up, for the Romans considered all lands as provinces of Rome.

This reshuffling of the Jewish cultural structure caused immense problems on multiple levels. As the Romans knew well, a fragmented society was easier to control, and posed less of a risk for a unified uprising or insurgency. As was to be expected, the once unified Jewish people became fragmented into four different groups.

[95] Sometimes referred to as a priest, a descendant of Aaron the Kohen mentioned in the Bible

The four groups of Jewish people:

Faced with the prospect of losing their Jewish culture and identity, and of becoming extinct, the Jewish people formed four unique ways to deal with this problem, and thus four unique groups formed.

1. Sadducees (Tzidukim in Hebrew) - wealthy Jews, the elite class.
2. Pharisees (Perushim in Hebrew) - Rabbis and Torah-observant Jews.
3. Essenes - Torah-observant Jews who ran away and hid in caves.
4. Zealots (Berunim in Aramaic) - Jews of various levels of observance; war-like in nature.

- For the Sadducees, their approach was complete capitulation to the Roman rule. After all their wealth made them powerful statesmen in the eyes of the Romans, and with it came extended privileges afforded only to Roman nobility.
- For the Pharisees, Roman rule was a major catastrophe. Not only was it a complete disgrace to the very nature of Judaism, it undermined the fabric of the Jewish way of life. However, the approach of the Pharisees was to try and be diplomatic in the hope of reaching some form of compromise, whereby Judaism could be preserved, albeit under the strict supervision of the Roman authorities.
- For the Essenes, the situation was entirely hopeless. The Essenes recognised that a compromised form of Judaism was meaningless. Knowing that they lacked the strength and ability to fight off the Romans, their best bet was to hide out in caves in an effort to preserve the untainted Jewish faith. Sadly, this group of Jews perished in what would later become known as the Bar Kochba Revolt.

- For the Zealots, fighting an enemy meant entertainment and action, to an otherwise ordinary life. The Zealots were keen on fighting the Romans, like many of the barbarian tribes who stood their ground, and fought to the bitter end.

According to the Talmud, Jesus was a rabbi in the group of Pharisees. Jesus had no intention of starting a new religion; his primary objective was actually to rebuke the other rabbi's, for allowing concessions with the Romans which would undermine what Judaism stood for.

What Jesus actually said, and how he intended to save Judaism is not known. We have no documents written by Jesus. But what is known; is the fact that Jesus only preached to Jews, concerning matters of Judaism.

What Jesus actually said, is not known. We have no documents written by Jesus.

Many rabbis of that period, tried to guide Judaism in its proper way, and tried to lead the Jewish people back to devout service of the Creator.

Thus one, who is not Jewish, has no connection to what Jesus or any other rabbi of that period had to say, because their intended audience was the Jewish people. It is almost ironic that a rabbi, who intended to save Judaism, resulted in being one of its greatest detractors.

The fall of the Roman Empire:

By around the year 300 CE, Rome faced constant threats, both locally and abroad. On the local front, there were many nobles vying for power, causing massive amounts of civil unrest. Abroad Rome was constantly being invaded by the barbarians.

By this time, the empire of Rome was split into an eastern and western segment, with two consuls for each segment.

It is very important to note, that the Romans had their own religion. The Romans were deeply attached to paganism. In fact, the ruler of that period, Diocletian made it compulsory for all Roman soldiers to pay tribute to the pagan gods prior to battle.

In the year 303 CE, Diocletian, passed new laws forbidding anyone from practicing the religion known as Christianity[96]. What Christianity was at that period, was not clear to its own observers. Many views, beliefs and practices existed all going by the name of Christianity.

Saul of Tarsus commonly known as St Paul, was also a rabbi and a contemporary of Jesus. What started out as a sect of Judaism was transformed by Paul.

Since Jesus only preached to Jews regarding matters about saving Judaism, his community was small, as only Jews had an interest in saving Judaism. However, the message of Jesus contained love, and hope, concepts which would be appealing to all people, especially the people subjugated under the Roman Empire. The majority of Roman subjects; had miserable lives, and were subjected to all forms of cruelty and humiliation. Thus a message of hope and salvation would have been incredibly inspiring.

Paul, knowing the message of Jesus was intended for Jews[97], was faced with a dilemma. On the one hand, the message of Jesus was only intended for Jews, since concepts such as the Sabbath, the Ten Commandments and nearly all the laws of the Old Testament[98], had no application for non-Jews. Thus the death of Jesus would bring an end to the message. On the other hand, the message of love and hope would be appealing to all people, and it would be a waste not to use the

[96] Lactantius, De Mortibus Persecutorum, X-XVI.
[97] Romans 2.19
[98] Referred to as the Nomos by Paul

teachings of Jesus to help the masses who were struggling with hopelessness[99].

Paul thus made the religion of Christianity, a new religion which would use the good parts of Jesus's inspirational teachings, and ignore what Jesus had to say to the Jews about strict Torah observance and faith in God.

Thus what Jesus actually said was lost, and Paul spread the message of love and hope to many people. Each audience heard that which they wanted to hear, and thus claimed to be Christian. What this system of beliefs was, was different, for different groups of people. The term Catholic coming from the Greek word catholicus, means universal. Paul thus created a universal religion, one that could be observed by all peoples.

As a rabbi, Paul was aware of the well-known Jewish law which states clearly, that in the end of time, there will be a saviour for the Jewish people[100].

The characteristics of this saviour were also well-known. According to Jewish law, in every generation a potential saviour of the Jews is born.

If an individual meets all the necessary criteria, that individual has the potential to be the saviour of the Jewish people. However, if the aforementioned individual dies, it is clear that he is not the saviour, of the end of time.

While Jesus was alive, many Jewish people were convinced that Jesus was the saviour. After Jesus died however, even the Jewish laymen knew Jesus could not possibly be the saviour. There have been many "false alarms" of the Jewish saviour, throughout Jewish history. Jesus was just one of many individuals, who was thought of as the saviour.

[99] Mathew 5-7
[100] Isaiah 59:20-21

Christianity is Chassidic in nature; there are many Chassidic sects of Jews today, who believe that their particular Rebbe (Master Teacher) is the saviour. In Jewish terms, Jesus was the first Chassidic Rebbe, and his followers would be termed Chassidim.

Every Chassid knows that once their Rebbe has died, he cannot possibly be the saviour. Paul must thus have struggled to keep Jesus's original Jewish congregants. It may be for this reason why it was said Jesus had not in fact died, and that he had been resurrected.

By the year 300 CE, Diocletian was well aware that the vast majorities of Romans, experienced the inequality of the times, and were hopelessly miserable. He even offered tax cuts to ease some of the suffering.

Diocletian hated Christianity for two reasons:

1. It was not the faith of the Roman culture.
2. The Christians by this time had attracted quite a substantial following, and thus posed a threat to the Roman rule. The Romans had learnt from Spartacus several centuries earlier, that if disgruntled individuals group together in unity, they can overthrow their superiors.

In the year 305 CE, Diocletian resigned from rule, being the first Roman Emperor to have ever done so. This heralded a new era in Rome, one sometimes referred to as the Dominate.

Diocletian's resignation left something of a power vacuum. Constantine who was raised by Diocletian, was disappointed when he was not selected as the successor and returned back to his father in the Western Empire. During this period, Maxentius usurped the Roman Empire. Maxentius was very popular among the common folk, as he claimed that he would give free grain to all. However, all his promises turned out to be lies.

In the year 306 CE, Constantine became the Emperor of the Western Empire, while Licinius was the Emperor of the Eastern Empire. Constantine and Licinius had opposing views on Christianity. Constantine was pro-Christian, whilst Licinius was anti-Christian. These opposing viewpoints became more apparent when the Goths of the Western Empire, which had support for Christianity, viewed Jesus as a non-human entity. The Goths in the Eastern Empire, who lacked support for Christianity, held a toned down approach and viewed Jesus as a mortal human being.

In the year 313 CE, Constantine issued the Edict of Milan[101] which allowed Christians to practice their faith in public. Constantine eventually overthrew Licinius, and he in turn became the sole ruler of the entire Roman Empire.

Constantine himself converted to Christianity, and set about on a mission to make Christianity the official religion of the Roman Empire. Having a single religion for the entire Empire would have been politically expedient, as this would have united the people, making them easier to govern.

As we stated earlier however, Christianity meant different things to different people, and before Constantine could spread Christianity as the official Roman religion, he had to formalise the religion itself. Constantine held an ecumenical council in Nicaea, a gathering of the leaders of all the differing forms of Christianity to sit together and form one unified version of what Christianity actually was.

In Nicaea, it was decided which texts should form the doctrine of Christianity. Some of the teachings of Jesus were not politically compatible and were thus scrapped from the final version. Some texts were useful but needed adjustment to best fit with the Roman ambitions. Questions such as "who is greater, Jesus or the Emperor?"

[101] Edward Gibbon, The History of the Decline and Fall of the Roman Empire, vol. III, Chapter XX.

needed answering. Perhaps this is why both the emperor and Jesus are referred to as "The son of God", i.e. one should respect both equally.

Thus the final version of the New Testament was created in Nicaea. Whether the New Testament was a product of Christianity or a political handbook, is a question that remains unanswered.

The New Testament and Old Testament, containing texts which were Roman-approved, and thoroughly edited, were combined together into a best-seller known today as the Bible.

In conclusion:

1. Jesus was a rabbi in Mesopotamia, and part of a group known as the Pharisees.
2. Christianity was started by Saul of Tarsus, but it was the Roman Emperor Constantine, who formalised Christianity into a religion.

12

THE NEW WORLD ORDER

The subject of the New World Order is one which has been viewed by many as a conspiracy theory, cloaked in mystery and reluctantly spoken about.

There is a great abundance of literature on the subject, some accurate and some entirely inaccurate and fabricated. Some authors spread information whilst others spread misinformation.

For our purposes, I would like to expand on this topic in a pragmatic way, without extraneous detail, with just the key information needed to grasp the subject, as it applies to those who are in search of the Creator.

The verse says[102]: "The heavens, the heavens are for the Creator, and the earth was given to man".

The Creator has allowed man to exert an incredible amount of influence on earth, using his free-will. Man has the power to influence either for good or for bad, the choice is his. Ultimately the Creator will remove the bad, and turn bad into good.

[102] Psalms 115

The philosophy behind the structure of dominance is based upon Roman culture, which values human worth upon material possessions.

The first thing one ought to know about the New World Order is that, it is not new.

In brief the "New World Order" is a concept, described by its Latin terminology "ORDO AB CHAO" (order from chaos).

Simply put the concept, is the idea of arranging the world into an orderly fashion. The new and orderly arrangement of the world is viewed as the ultimate state of world affairs.

The first thing one ought to know about the New World Order is that, it is not new

Thus one could state that there exists an "Old World" which is characterised by chaos, and the "New World" which is characterised by order.

The method used to accomplish the new and more orderly world, is by means of creating chaos in the world.

For example: if one wished to create a new nuclear power station in a particular region; one would first need to create the associated chaos, namely a perceived lack of power, within that region. Once the perceived lack of power is out of hand and "chaotic", a solution of a new nuclear power station in the region is introduced.

Thus the new world is not simply a re-organisation of that which is, but rather a deliberate steering of world events, based upon the problem, reaction and, solution technique.

The ultimate goal is thus, for the world to be run in an organised manner. Those doing the organisation and setting the rules are known as the enlightened ones.

These enlightened ones, are thought of as the best and brightest amongst the human race. It is only fitting therefore, that if the world is going to be set in order, those doing the setting must be the best that the human race has to offer, much like the pilot in the cockpit is the most suitable person to be in control, from among all those on board.

The concepts as will be elaborated further on, are in fact thousands of years old, and have existed ever since man first set foot on planet Earth.

To understand this topic, we will need to explore history and the basic nature of the human condition.

Since the dawn of civilisation, mankind has been driven by lust, jealousy and arrogance. It is in the nature of the human being to lust after pleasure, power and honour.

In very simple terms, we can refer to Maslow's hierarchy of needs, which gives us an understanding of what motivates the human being to act. The first desire or need is physiological such as food and shelter. Once these desires have been met, the human being seeks security, followed by social and emotional needs.

As the human population increased over time, an interesting phenomenon emerged. As the number of human beings increased on planet Earth, we learnt about the various character traits which can emerge from the human species. One of the traits which emerged, seemingly built into the fabric of human nature, was the desire for one human being to control another.

Very often this trait lays dormant, or is suppressed due to the inability of the individual to overtly express this trait. On occasion this desire manifests, and is controlled by the individual in a positive manner. More often than not however, when this desire manifests, it takes ahold of the individual, and incapacitates them from rational thought and human emotion.

To quote the words of John Emerich Edward Dalberg-Acton, 1st Baron Acton;

"Power tends to corrupt, and absolute power corrupts absolutely. Great men are almost always bad men."[103]

In early civilisations, human beings gathered together to form a tribe. In most cases, the tribe would have a tribal leader. The tribal leader is the manifestation of this human trait namely the desire of one human to control another, or in this case a group of others.

A tribe may have grown, due to conquering another tribe, or by means of amalgamation with another tribe. This larger tribe may have formed a village, and later a town, and later still a city.

This process has repeated itself in all parts of the world since the beginning of human civilisation, and has brought us to where we stand today as the human race.

Like bacteria in a Petri dish, we as the human species have multiplied, mutated and grown to occupy our planet. We have cities and countries today, but we are in fact just one large tribe of humans settling on planet Earth.

We often find among many animal species, that becoming the head of the pack, involves fighting with other contenders, to gain a respected position of dominance. True tribal leaders are created in the human species in a similar fashion.

Thus for millennia, the human animal has also been fighting, to gain a position of dominance.
The trait of controlling other members of the species is not unique to the human being.

[103] Letter to Bishop Mandell Creighton, April 5, 1887 published in Historical Essays and Studies, edited by J. N. Figgis and R. V. Laurence (London: Macmillan, 1907)

The agenda[104] of the New World Order is thus based upon tribalism, with the ultimate goal of forming a single world tribe, with a single tribal leader.

How a tribal leader is made:

As is the case in the animal kingdom, the leader demonstrates strength over all other members in the group.

The members in the group do not "elect" their leader, but rather the leader asserts his/her dominance over the herd, and thus exerts authority over the other members.

Among the human species, strength or dominance is shown in the form of wealth. Thus a wealth fight ensues, with the wealthiest human declaring him/herself as the leader of the pack.

The importance of globalisation[105]:

Just as it is better to be the leader of two tribes rather than one, so too it is better to be the leader of the entire village and so on.

To this end, the ultimate agenda of the New World Order is to form the biggest country ever, this country will be called planet Earth. Thus the ultimate form of one human being controlling another is to have one world with one leader.

The fight for world domination has been taking place for many centuries; we are getting closer each day to having a New World, a world without countries with open borders and mixed populations.

[104] See Agenda 21 and Agenda 30 for further details of the plan.

[105] See the Novel by Aldous Huxley entitled Brave New World (London, 1932) based on non-fiction.

Who is in the race?

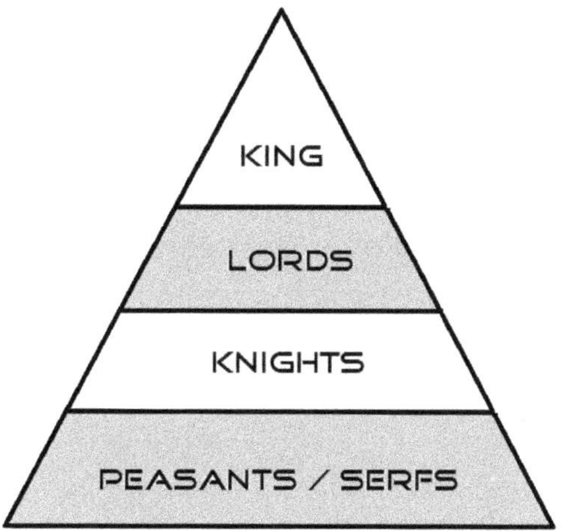

The race to become world leader is fought amongst the upper class, i.e. the strongest members of the human race.

This concept is known as the feudal system. The feudal system of the 15th century was based upon land ownership. Those with the greatest wealth in the form of land ownership were known as monarchs such as kings and queens, Monarchs were the highest tier in the feudal system.

Beneath the monarchs we find people possessing smaller land holdings. These groups of individuals in the second tier were known as "lords" or "vassals", who were subservient to the reigning monarch.

In the third tier, there were "knights" who were also vassals subservient to the monarch. The knight had value, as he could provide security to the classes above him. The services of a knight were often paid for, in parcels of land or gold. Thus a valiant knight could potentially become a lord, during his career in protection of the king.

The lowest class, namely the fourth tier of individuals, was known as "peasants" or "serfs". This group of individuals enjoyed little to no status in the kingdom. However, they provided value to the kingdom as a whole, mostly through their labour in the production of food. The peasant would endeavour to become a knight, as this would elevate his status within the kingdom.

Therefore in brief, the feudal system is a system of top-down control. Those at the top possessed all the wealth, which would be exchanged with the lower classes for goods and services, such as food and protection.

The feudal system continued throughout the centuries. The names of the various tiers have changed over the years however.

For example, today we don't refer to the lowest tier as peasants or serfs, but rather workers or something similar.

The terms have also changed over the years, but the concepts are identical. For example we don't refer to those who work without adequate compensation, as "slaves" or being "enslaved", but rather call these individuals "employed".

In my opinion the modern feudal system is still in place. With the change in names of who is subservient to who, I call the modern feudal system, the "Practical Class System".

The Practical Class System or modern feudal system is identical to the medieval feudal system in Europe. For clarity sake, I have divided the tiers into terms we are familiar with today namely, upper class, middle class and lower class. I have drawn this opinion from the nature of the human being, as well as the common traits found in all generations. The assertion is that power struggles will always exist in the background of any civilization. Power struggles will revolve around what a society attributes power to. As such the groupings discussed are theoretical in nature, and the discourse revolves around conceptual elements.

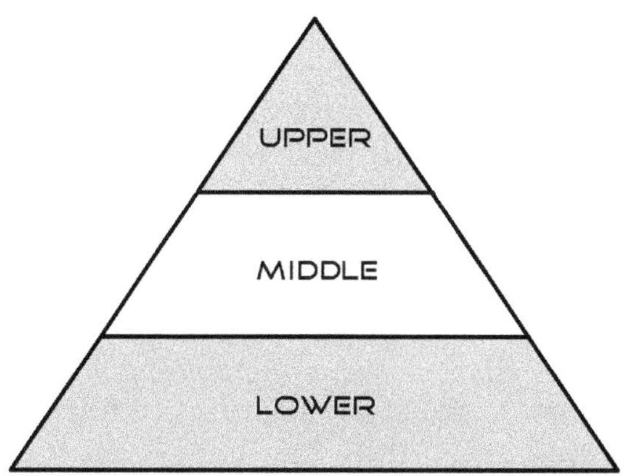

PRACTICAL CLASS SYSTEM

UPPER CLASS:

- People with an unknown net worth, often exceeding trillions of $US.[106]

MIDDLE CLASS:

- People with a net worth between 1 billion $US and 1 trillion $US

LOWER CLASS:

- People with a net worth less than 1 billion $US

An important point must be drawn to attention: just as the old feudal system viewed the lowest tier of humanity as chattel (items which can be bought and sold, such as slaves); so too in the practical class system.

[106] $US have been used simply for the clarification of the vast extent of wealth in 2018 terms. There is no definitive demarcation at the trillion mark, but serves as an indicator. For example an individual who has a net worth of $US 500 Billion may be included in the upper classes if he/she is not a public figure.

1. **The upper class**: This is a group of people who prefer to remain discreet, due to their great power and influence. These are monarch families, that are centuries old, and are the legal land owners of entire countries.
2. **The middle class**: is a larger group of people who are ruled by the upper class. Unlike the upper class, the middle class is well known to the public, by name and occupation.
3. **The lower class:** consists of all other living creatures, including "poor" people and wildlife. The value of a "lower class" human being is no more valuable than that of an insect <u>in this system</u>. The lower class can be indiscriminately eradicated without fear or consequence. Akin to deforestation, or the eradication of unwanted rodents.

The feudal system:

The feudal system both past and present is a top-down approach to controlling worldwide events, to steer the human race in a particular direction.

In my opinion, for many years, social experiments have been conducted aimed at genetic research and depopulation in the name of establishing a "New World Order". Some of these include: The "Spanish flu"[107], the Holocaust and Nazism[108] as well as apartheid in South Africa[109], to name but a few.

[107] January 1918 – December 1920 affecting 500 million people
[108] 1939-1945 affecting 100 million people
[109] 1948-1994 affecting 50 million people

In more recent times we have seen other wars, as well as the push for:

- One border - Open borders
- One culture - Cultural erosion
- One currency
- One gender
- One language
- One race
- One religion

All of the above makes it easier to control the intended system.

As with any concept, there are both positive and negative aspects of the "New World Order".

Positive aspects:

- If the leader of human civilisation is absolutely pious in every imaginable way, and does not possess any character flaws, such as greed, lust, dishonesty or arrogance; then such a leader may in fact be a positive thing for the human race.

- Having one unified world, can also be an extremely positive force on the human race. If the world population was able to join forces and act as one collective unit, this would be an incredible and unstoppable force.

- Having a man-made ruler can be positive, provided that the overlord rules with humility and love, and creates peace among human beings.

If the aforementioned overlord rules his subjects in a dignified manner, without oppression and for the sake of his subjects and not his/her own benefit, then such an overlord can be an ambassador of the human race to the Creator.

In the current state of affairs the top-down approach has had horrific consequences, and has caused immense suffering to the human population. In my opinion, many authority figures are currently leading the masses to their demise, like sheep to the slaughter.

Many authority figures are currently leading the masses to their demise, like sheep to the slaughter.

The culling of the human race should be done in a dignified manner, and the masses should be informed of the agenda to depopulate the planet.

Unfortunately, the social experiments conducted in the past; to curtail the human population were done in a brutal and undignified manner.

Every human being has the right to die in a dignified manner, and at a time and place of his/her choosing, in a manner which is neither painful nor humiliating.

Negative aspects:

- **Propaganda and deceit:** Deliberately misleading the masses, using deceit, to both hide, and avoid the ill consequences. This includes Human rights abuse: In some regions of the world, human beings are overtly stripped of their human rights. In other regions of the world, which claim to have human rights, these rights are slowly but surely being abolished, usually **under the guise of a false meme or narrative**, and using pleasant sounding words such as "sustainable", "environment", "diversified", "neutrality" etc.

- **Planting seeds of hatred:** Deliberately causing tension and hatred between races, cultures, genders, religions and families, for the sake of weakening the population - using the Roman technique of "divide and conquer".

- **False Democracy**: Many individuals to this day still believe that their mark on a ballot paper has some bearing as to who is appointed as a head of state. Too few are aware that the Roman "Senate" selects heads of state often years in advance.

- **Transparency:** Too few are aware that the role of "government" is merely as a functionary tool. Much like a farm owner employs a farm worker, to deal with the mess made by the cattle, so too "governments" are employed to deal with the mess made by the lower class chattel.

The current agenda of the "New World Order" spells absolute misery for more than 90% of the world's population.

Furthermore: due to the fact that the current agenda, values the human being solely on a monetary basis, and not on any substantive measurement it is prone to failure.

Moreover, due to the fact that the concept of the "New World Order" is driven by negative human traits such as lust and jealousy, the few survivors will ultimately become victims of betrayal and live in constant fear of losing power and authority. Thus the idea is doomed at its end point.

In closing:
Although the Creator has given man free will, and has allowed human beings to exert their dominance over others, this is not beneficial for mankind. The Creator wants mankind to be free and only subservient to the Creator, not to man. Man is free to choose however, and the Creator allows humans to be subservient should they so desire.
As the Creator said to the prophet Samuel: (Versus 7-22)

"The Creator said to Samuel; Listen to the voice of the people in all that they say to you, for it is not you whom they have rejected, but it is me whom they have rejected from reigning over them."[110]

[110] Samuel 1 8:7-22

Furthermore we see that the nature of mankind is to rule over others with brutality and cruelty. This is not something new, but can be clearly seen in the book of Amos, dating back to around 750 BCE.

> "Hear this prophecy, you cows of Bashan[111] who are on the mountain of Samaria, who oppress the poor and crush the destitute…."[112]

One, who is searching for the Creator, may often reject the very notion of the existence of the Creator, feeling let down, disappointed and even angry that the Creator is not more engaging and helpful.
However one should rather lose faith in humanity. The birth of a misanthrope begins with the realisation, that it is humanity and not the Creator which has failed.

No human being can act against the ultimate plan of the Creator himself.

Not knowing when an event is the act of the Creator, and when it is an act of a human being, can be one of the most challenging obstacles for those who seek the Creator.

Knowing that what the Creator desires and what the Creator allows to occur, are two very different and sometimes opposite things.

However one must always bear in mind that despite the untold suffering caused by human beings, no human being can act against the ultimate plan of the Creator himself.

Losing faith in man is a key step in gaining faith in the Creator.

The Roman culture, of hoarding and lording wealth is a form of the mental illness, known as obsessive-compulsive disorder. Hoarding refers to obsessing over money and trying to collect as much as possible, whereas as lording, refers to using this accumulated wealth to buy control over others.

---

[111] A reference to the elite

[112] Amos 4:1

As was seen by the fall of the Roman Empire, using wealth as a barometer of human value, leads to complete and utter destruction.

A dignified human being should aspire, to use his/her wealth for the benefit of humanity. In Japan, CEOs of large corporations are ashamed to draw large salaries, as the Japanese culture frowns upon greed, as opposed to the Roman culture.

If one's wealth is accumulating beyond reason, this is a sign that the wealth is being hoarded and not spent on the betterment of humanity.

Wealth which is being used appropriately is never "stuck"; it is constantly on the move, improving the lives of others.

An accumulation or buildup, of excessive personal wealth is a sign that this wealth is not flowing freely. A buildup of personal wealth is as dangerous as a buildup of fatty deposits on the walls of the arteries. Like blood, wealth should be free-flowing at all times.

Philanthropy - Kindness or facade:

Philanthropy is a popular term used to mask the underlying greed and selfishness which is found with hoarders.

Philanthropy is a tokenism of true empathy, and is a term used when one gives a miniscule portion of one's wealth to another.

One who is kind-hearted and generous, would give a significant percentage of one's wealth for the betterment of others.

I view the term philanthropist as an insult. One who calls him/herself a philanthropist may as well call him/herself a pedophile, it is nothing to be proud of.

Generosity is measured in the percentage ratio, rather than in the amount given. For example:

- Mr. X has a net worth of 1000 and gives 10, or 1%
- Mr. Y has a net worth of 100 and gives 10 or 10%

Mr. Y is 10 times more generous, than Mr. X. Even though both Mr. X and Mr. Y gave the same amount, the comparative percentage ratio of 1% to 10% is how we measure the nature of the generosity. 10% is a significant percentage whereas 1% is not.

Perhaps one of the greatest scars left by Roman culture was the need to attain fame through one's wealth. If one does acquire vast wealth, this should not be known to others. Furthermore if one uses his/her wealth in the appropriate manner by helping others to achieve success, this too should be a private matter.

One who finds it necessary; to make known what charitable deeds they have done is in most instances displaying a form of narcissism.

The story of Albert - *A short story as a parable - Taking credit for half fixing a problem,* ***you caused*** *in the first place:*

My name is Albert.

Several years ago, I started a free wheelchair lending service. This service provides the use of a wheelchair, to anyone who is unable to walk, absolutely free of charge, no questions asked.

My wheelchair lending service, has gained widespread popularity, and has given me a reputation within my community, as being a generous, kind and philanthropic individual.

I have appeared in several newspaper articles, as well as on radio and TV. I love the honour and respect I am given, nothing quite satisfies my ego, like the praise and compliments of others.

The attention I receive, makes me feel validated as a person, and is entwined in the very fabric of my personality. Today I receive honour and praise wherever I go, be it a public gathering or even a social event. I am always made to feel important, noteworthy and a shining example of what philanthropy is all about.

But things were not always this way. When I first started out, I had just a few wheelchairs and the phone hardly ever rang. I would sit for days and weeks, waiting for someone, anyone to call and ask to borrow a wheelchair. The situation was so desperate that even a mere query would brighten the gloomy day.

Then suddenly, I was struck with inspiration. If I wanted the honour and attention I so desperately desired, I had to increase the demand for wheelchair users.
With my goals firmly set, I handpicked five drivers, and gave them the task of finding pedestrians to knock over. I specifically instructed the drivers not to kill the pedestrians, but merely to give them a good ramming, enough to ensure that they would require a wheelchair in the not too distant future.

The drivers set out on the roads, and my operation began to swing into full force. Drivers were given targets to reach each month, and without fail, every target was met. Before long, the phone was ringing non-stop, business was booming and I employed another twelve drivers. Within the first six months of implementing my new approach, I was already receiving notoriety. Cards were pouring in by the dozen, singing my praises and hailing me as a local hero.

From humble beginnings, I have built a solid reputation as being a great philanthropist. There is almost no building and almost no individual in my community which hasn't been touched by my great work.

Recently, one of my drivers, accidently killed a pedestrian. At first I was in shock and horror, as this type of mishap had never occurred before. Out of a sense of guilt, and as a show of upholding my good standing in the community, I attended the funeral of this particular individual.

To my amazement, I was given even more honour and respect by the entire community. I even overheard people saying "Albert is such an amazing person, so caring and compassionate".

I was given red carpet treatment for lowering myself, to attend the funeral of some random nobody. Not only was I given the esteem of being such a giver, but even the credit for being so humble in my philanthropic work.

I have now started a second service, visiting the injured in hospital and attending the occasional funeral, things couldn't be going better.

I am enjoying life, and making a real difference in the world, the only part I don't share with the media and the public at large, is my secret to success. I have never told anybody that all it takes is a few drivers, and a passion to bolster your public image.

In conclusion:

The Creator made wealth as a tool for mankind. Unfortunately mainly due to Roman culture, mankind has abused this tool, and used it to harm his fellow human being.

- Wealth is neither good, nor bad it is simply a tool. In the right hands, the tool can be used for good.
- Wealth is not the barometer of human value.
- Kindness and generosity is measured by a percentage ratio.
- No human being can disrupt the ultimate plan of the Creator.

13

THE TALMUD

In your search for the Creator, you will most likely encounter the Judaic texts of the Talmud. For some reason many individuals who either know that there is a Creator, but despise the Creator, have taken issue with the Talmud. One can always spot an atheist in the making when one encounters an individual who disparages others from Torah study.

Rashi comments[113] that there are 7 steps one leading to the next, which brings a person to denying the Creator.

1. He does not study
2. He does not perform
3. He disapproves of others who do perform
4. He hates the Sages
5. He prevents others from performing the commandments
6. He denies that the commandments were commanded by the Creator.
7. He denies the Creator's existence

[113] Leviticus – Vayikra 26:15

In this section we will explore the Talmud, and answer questions such as:

- "What is the Talmud?"
- "What is the Talmud about?"
- "When was the Talmud written?"
- "Why is the Talmud sometimes viewed with hostility?"

What is the Talmud?

Many years ago, when I first began teaching Adult Educational classes, a student asked me, "Where can I get a copy of the Talmud?" His assumption was, that the Talmud was a hundred page reader, filled with Jewish thoughts and ideas. However, he soon discovered, that the Talmud is not a single book, but rather a set of books containing 63 volumes, 5422 pages (or 2711 daf[114]) and when studied one folio per day, takes seven-and-a-half years to complete.

To study an entire folio every day, 365 days a year is quite challenging, and in a more practical sense, a single page a day is usually more appropriate for first-time-students. Thus the Talmud is a set of works which takes 15 years to read.

There are few, if any books, today which take 15 years just to read.

Apart from the immense scale of the Talmud, there are also hundreds of thousands of commentaries and super-commentaries[115] on the Talmud. Thus to study the Talmud requires approximately 1,000,000 pages of reading.

To put that into perspective, that would mean reading all of Shakespeare's works of 37 plays, and 154 poems, several times over.

[114] A daf or folio is a double sided page

[115] A super commentary is a commentary about a commentary

But that is not all, there are approximately 1,000,000 pages just relating to the Babylonian Talmud, there is also the Jerusalem Talmud and several variations of the Babylonian Talmud.

A conservative estimate would put all the works of the Talmud and their related commentaries in the region of approximately 2,000,000 pages.

Thus the Talmud is a life-long study project covering 2,000,000 (two million) pages of literature. A Talmudic scholar would typically spend 20 years of full-time study, to master the Talmud and its teachings.

What is the Talmud about?

The Talmud is essentially the corpus of Jewish literature, encompassing every aspect of Jewish life, including Jewish law, Jewish ethics and Jewish stories and history. The Talmud forms part of the Oral Torah.
In Judaism, the Torah is divided into two distinct segments:

The written Torah, consisting of:

- **The Five Books of Moses**:
  - Bereishis - Genesis
  - Shmos - Exodus
  - Vayikra - Leviticus
  - Bamidbar - Numbers
  - Devarim - Deuteronomy
- **The Eight Books of Prophets** (including the 12 Minor Prophets)
  - Yehoshua - Joshua
  - Shoftim - Judges

- Shmuel - Samuel
- Melachim - Kings
- Yishiah - Isaiah
- Yirmiyah - Jeremiah
- Yecheskiel - Ezekiel
- Hoshia - Hosea
- Yoel - Joel
- Amos - Amos
- Ovadyah - Obadiah
- Yona - Jonah
- Micha - Micah
- Nachum - Nahum
- Chavakook - Habakkuk
- Tzafania - Zephaniah

There were numerous Jewish prophets; some prophets received the instruction to write down their prophecy, while others did not. Usually we find the text indicating the instruction to write with the words: "So says God." etc.

Only the prophets, who were instructed to write, form the books of prophets. The oral tradition states the reason the prophet was instructed to write, was due to the fact that the message would be relevant for all times.

- **The Eleven Books of Writings:**

The books of writings were not written with prophecy, but with a **lower spiritual awakening** called Ruach Ha-Kodesh (Holy Spirit)[116].

The period of "Writings" ended around 400 BC, with the final book chronologically, being the book of Ester. All the explanations and commentary were not written down, but rather formed the "Oral Torah."

The Eleven Books written with Ruach Ha-Kodesh are:

- Tehillim - Psalms
- Mishlei - Proverbs
- Iyov - Job
- Shir Ha Shirim - Song of Songs
- Rus - Ruth
- Eicha - Lamentations
- Koheles - Ecclesiastes
- Ester - Esther
- Daniel - Daniel
- Ezra and Nechemya - Ezra-Nehemiah
- Divrei Ha Yomim - Chronicles

These Eleven Books were not just selected, as popular literature, but rather as was the case with the prophets, these eleven books were given, with the instruction to be written.

[116] See: The Way of God, Rabbi Moshe Chaim Luzzatto, Translated by Aryeh Kaplan, Feldheim, Jerusalem, 6th ed, 1999, pp 221-245.

These and only these 24 books may be written in Jewish law. Anything apart from these books forms part of the "Oral Torah".

The written Torah is often called the "**Tanach**" which is an acronym for:

1. Torah (the Five Books of Moses)
2. Ne'veim (the Eight Books of Prophets)
3. Kesuvim (the Eleven Books of Writings)

The "**Tanach**" consists of 24 books, containing approximately 22, 098 (twenty-two thousand and ninety-eight) verses.

The verses themselves are referred to as the "Written Torah", as technically speaking only these verses may be written down according to Jewish law.

The "Oral Torah", may not be written down however. It was only sanctioned due to severe circumstances, as we will discuss shortly.

The verses in the "Tanach" appear to read like something of a story, but upon closer inspection it becomes rather obvious that these verses cannot be understood without commentaries.

The mere wording and syntax makes these documents unreadable, and without a doubt impossible to translate. All translations of the "**Tanach**" are renditions based upon commentary.
Having a command of biblical Hebrew, is essential to making head or tail of these writings.

There are numerous commentaries and super-commentaries on the written Torah, also in the region of 2,000,000 (two million) pages. The work of Rashi[117] is often viewed as the starting point to understanding these texts. The commentary of Rashi is based upon the Oral Tradition, found within the Oral Torah.

[117] Rabbi Shlomo ben Yitzach

The "Oral Torah"[118]:

The "Oral Torah" is viewed as the "key" to understanding the "Written Torah". Jewish tradition states that Moses received both the "Written Torah" and the "Oral Torah" on Mount Sinai. The "Oral Torah" has been passed down and taught from generation to generation, in an unbroken chain, for almost 3500 years.

The primary categories of the "Oral Torah" can be divided into four segments.

1. Mishna
2. Gemora
3. Rishonim
4. Achronim

All of these serve as a commentary to the written Torah, thus the Oral Torah is the oral tradition of Judaism.

Despite being called the Oral Torah, as opposed to written Torah, from the year 100 CE (approximately), the oral traditions of Judaism were written down, as will be explained further on.

The Talmud is thus one of the segments of the Oral Torah, and forms part of the oral tradition in Judaism. It would be difficult to say exactly how many books exist today as a part of the Oral Torah, but an estimate would place it somewhere in the region of 1,000,000 (one million) books, varying in size.

To know the entire written and oral Torah would entail, a study of approximately 100,000,000 (one hundred million) pages of text.

This vast amount of information, would take a lifetime of study to even scratch the surface of understanding. Being a Torah scholar is a full

[118] Fundamentals of Judaism, Michael Eljarrat, 2014, USA

time occupation, requiring immense dedication and focus, as the corpus of literature is almost beyond comprehension.

The subjects covered in the Talmud:

The Talmud is made up of two components:

1. The Mishna - written in Hebrew
2. The Gemora - written in Aramaic

The Mishna: comprises of six "Orders" dealing; with specific Jewish laws[119]:

1. Zeraryim - The laws of agriculture.
2. Mo'ed - The laws of Shabbos and Jewish holidays.
3. Nashim - The laws of marriage and divorce.
4. Ne'zekin - The laws of monetary matters.
5. Kodshim - The laws of sacrifices.
6. Te'haros - The laws of ritual impurities.

The Mishna is written in an unelaborated manner without discussion or commentary.

The Gemora:

The Gemora is a discussion, and an elaboration of the text dealt with in the Mishna. The modern-day Talmud has the Mishna and Gemora printed into a single volume. Each volume of the Talmud is known as a tractate[120].

[119] Known as Sedorim – Orders
[120] Masechta – In Aramaic

These are the tractates found within the Babylonian Talmud, divided into its six "Orders":

In the order of Zerayim:

1. Berachos **(Talmud 64 Daf / Folio or 128 pages)** (dealing with blessings)
2. Pe'ah - No Talmud only Mishna (dealing with special tithes)
3. Demai - No Talmud only Mishna (dealing with questionable tithes)
4. Kil'ayim - No Talmud only Mishna (dealing with grafting of species)
5. Shevi'is - No Talmud only Mishna (dealing with the Sabbatical Year called Sh'mita)
6. Terumos - No Talmud only Mishna (dealing with tithes for the Kohen - Jewish priest)
7. Ma'aseros - No Talmud only Mishna (dealing with tithes for the Levites)
8. Ma'aser Sheni - No Talmud only Mishna (dealing with secondary tithes)
9. Challah - No Talmud only Mishna (dealing with a gift of bread given to the Kohen- Jewish priest)

10. Orlah - No Talmud only Mishna (dealing with the laws of prohibited fruit produces)

11. Bikkurim - No Talmud only Mishna (dealing with the first fruits given to the Kohen- Jewish priest)

In the order of Mo'ed:

1. Shabbos **(Talmud 157 Daf / Folio or 314 pages)** (dealing with the laws of Shabbos)
2. Eruvin **(Talmud 105 Daf / Folio or 210 pages)** (dealing with domains on Shabbos)
3. Pesachim **(Talmud 121 Daf / Folio or 242 pages)** (dealing with the laws of Passover)
4. Shekalim **(Talmud 22 Daf / Folio or 44 pages)** (dealing with the laws of the Half-Shekel)
5. Rosh Hashana **(Talmud 35 Daf / Folio or 70 pages)** (dealing with the laws of Rosh Hashana)
6. Yoma **(Talmud 88 Daf / Folio or 176 pages)** (dealing with the laws of Yom Kippur)
7. Sukkah **(Talmud 56 Daf / Folio or 112 pages)** (dealing with the laws of Succa)
8. Beitza **(Talmud 40 Daf / Folio or 80 pages)** (dealing with the laws of Yom Tov)
9. Ta'anis **(Talmud 31 Daf / Folio or 62 pages)** (dealing with the laws of fast days)
10. Megillah **(Talmud 32 Daf / Folio or 64 pages)** (Dealing with the laws of Purim)

11. Mo'ed Katan **(Talmud 29 Daf / Folio or 58 pages)** (dealing with the laws of Chol Ha Moed)
12. Chagigah **(Talmud 27 Daf / Folio or 54 pages)** (dealing with the laws of festival sarifices)

In the order of Nashim:

1. Yevomos **(Talmud 122 Daf / Folio or 244 pages)** (dealing with sibling marriage)
2. Kesubos **(Talmud 112 Daf / Folio or 224 pages)** (dealing with marriage contracts)
3. Nedarim **(Talmud 91 Daf / Folio or 182 pages)** (dealing with the laws of vows)
4. Nazir **(Talmud 66 Daf / Folio or 132 pages)** (dealing with the laws of the nazir)
5. Sotah **(Talmud 49 Daf / Folio or 98 pages)** (dealing with the laws of an adulterer)
6. Gittin **(Talmud 90 Daf / Folio or 180 pages)** (dealing with the laws of divorce)
7. Kiddushin **(Talmud 82 Daf / Folio or 164 pages)** (dealing with the laws of marriage)

In the order of Ne'zekin:

1. Bava Kamma **(Talmud 119 Daf / Folio or 238 pages)** (dealing with the laws of damages)
2. Bava Metzia **(Talmud 119 Daf / Folio or 238 pages)** (dealing with the laws of lost articles)
3. Bava Basra **(Talmud 176 Daf / Folio or 352 pages)** (dealing with the laws of property rights)
4. Sanhedrin **(Talmud 113 Daf / Folio or 226 pages)** (dealing with the laws of Jewish Courts)
5. Makkos **(Talmud 24 Daf / Folio or 48 pages)** (dealing with the laws of testimony)
6. Shevu'os **(Talmud 49 Daf / Folio or 98 pages)** (dealing with the laws of oaths)
7. Avodah Zarah **(Talmud 76 Daf / Folio or 152 pages)** (dealing with the laws of idolatry)
8. Horayos **(Talmud 14 Daf / Folio or 28 pages)** (dealing with judicial mistakes)
9. Ediyos - No Talmud only Mishna (Dealing with the laws of various measurements)
10. Avos - No Talmud only Mishna dealing with ethics.

In the order of Kodshim:

1. Zevachim **(Talmud 120 Daf / Folio or 240 pages)** (dealing with the laws of animal sacrifices)
2. Menachos **(Talmud 110 Daf / Folio or 220 pages)** (dealing with the laws of flour offerings)
3. Chullin **(Talmud 142 Daf / Folio or 284 pages)** (dealing with the laws of Kosher)
4. Bechoros **(Talmud 61 Daf / Folio or 122 pages)** (dealing with the laws of the firstborn)
5. Arychin **(Talmud 34 Daf / Folio or 68 pages)** (dealing with the laws of valuations)
6. Temurah **(Talmud 34 Daf / Folio or 68 pages)** (dealing with the laws of sacrificial exchanges)
7. Kerisos **(Talmud 28 Daf / Folio or 56 pages)** (dealing with the laws of Kares)
8. Me'ilah **(Talmud 22 Daf / Folio or 44 pages)** (dealing with the laws of misappropriation)
9. Kinnim **(Talmud 25 Daf / Folio or 50 pages)** (dealing with sacrificial mistakes)
10. Tamid **(Talmud 33 Daf / Folio or 66 pages)** (dealing with the daily sacrifice in the Temple)

11. Middos – 37 Daf / Folio or 74 pages, no Talmud only Mishna (dealing with conduct)

In the order of Te'haros:

1. Keilim - No Talmud only Mishna (dealing with ritual impurity on vessels)
2. Oholot - No Talmud only Mishna (dealing with ritual impurity caused by a corpse)
3. Nega'im - No Talmud only Mishna (dealing with ritual impurity caused by contact)
4. Parah – No Talmud only Mishna (dealing with the "Red Heifer")
5. Tohoros - No Talmud only Mishna (dealing with the laws of purity)
6. Mikva'os - No Talmud only Mishna (dealing with the laws of a ritual bath)
7. Niddah **(Talmud 73 Daf / Folio or 146 pages)** (dealing with the laws of family purity)
8. Makshirin - No Talmud only Mishna (dealing with the laws of preparation for impurity)
9. Zavim - No Talmud only Mishna (dealing with the laws impurity of bodily fluids)

10. Tevul Yom - No Talmud only Mishna (dealing with the laws of light impurities)

11. Yadayim - No Talmud only Mishna (dealing with the laws of hand impurities)

12. Uktzim - - No Talmud only Mishna (dealing with the laws of fruit and vegetable impurities)

The Talmud is essentially a foundational corpus of literature dealing with Jewish law. Unlike the doctrines found in other religions, the written and Oral Torah are concerned with what Jews need to practice in order to fulfil their mandate of Judaism.

Jewish law mandates, that every Jewish male is obligated to know the entire written and Oral Torah.

Both the written and Oral Torah only devote approximately 3% of their contents, to how Jews are to conduct themselves towards non-Jews.

As a side point, it was this very fact that concerned Saul of Tarsus (Saint Paul), when presenting the Torah to non-Jews, since the "Nomos" laws pertain only to Jews and have no relevance to non-Jews.

In Judaism, non-Jews are not obligated to study the Torah, and are not obligated to keep any of the 613 commandments.

The Torah is a guideline for Jews to practise Judaism.

From a Jewish perspective, non-Jews are strongly discouraged from converting to Judaism, since a Jew is obligated to adhere to 613 commandments. Such a great undertaking is not appropriate for everyone.

In Judaism non-Jews have 7 rules to follow.

The Ten Commandments for example, are not universal principles for mankind, but rather Ten Commandments for Jews, apart from another 603 commandments, which are also only applicable to Jews.

As we will discuss shortly, there is a great misconception about what the Talmud is, and for numerous reasons, the Talmud has gained a reputation amongst non-Jews, as being discriminate and antagonistic towards non-Jews. In actual fact only 3% is even directed at non-Jews, and when understood in context, is not discriminatory or antagonistic to non-Jews.

Just as Hindu or Buddhist literature, is intended for a Hindu to practice Hinduism or the Buddhist to practice Buddhism respectively, so too is Jewish literature intended for Jews to practice Judaism.

The parts of Jewish literature which deal with a non-Jew are entirely inconsequential. However owing to the fact that Judaism is often treated with utmost contempt and repulsion; many works in Jewish literature have been portrayed in a negative light.

Even my own work "Fundamentals of Judaism" has been criticised, as trying "to convert non-Jews to Judaism". Nothing could be further from the truth.

In fact, one of the motivations behind this work is to distil the parts of Jewish literature which are applicable to all human beings, and to separate from that which is applicable only to Jews.

In Judaism, one doesn't need to be a Jew to be a good person.

Judaism has a more holistic view of humanity, and does not compel any individual to convert to Judaism. A non-Jew has to follow seven rules that were given to Adam and Noah. Apart from those rules, a non-Jew is absolutely free to do as he/she pleases.

Not only is conversion discouraged, but one who converts for any motive, other than for the desire to practice Judaism, as a Jew, i.e. to study and practice the "Written Torah" and "Oral Torah" is not considered a convert.

Although today, anyone with a pulse and some money can become "Jewish" this is an adulteration of the essence of Judaism, and one of the many corruptions found within our society.

Judaism is not for everyone; it is a lifestyle choice for those who wish to be persecuted and hated by the world.

Practising Judaism requires enormous amounts of devotion, lifestyle changes and commitment to adhere to the faith under all circumstances. If you are looking for a challenge, rather climb Mount Everest, naked and barefoot.

On the other hand one who is devoted to practising authentic Judaism, i.e. one who is compelled to study the "Written Torah" and the "Oral Torah" with sincerity and emotional intelligence, and to practise Judaism as a Jew, is seen as a tremendously pious individual.

Unlike Roman culture which places the value of a human being, on his/her financial net worth, Judaism places value on striving to be a good person.

Your value in society is measured by your concern for the well-being of others, regardless of your background.

As the Talmud states[121]:

Rabbi Meir would say: From where do we know that even a "star worshipper" who toils in Torah that he (has the status) like a High Priest?

From the verse which says [Leviticus 18:5] "Which **a man** shall do and live"
The verse does not say Priests, Levites or Israelites but rather a man, (any man Jewish or not).

[121] Avoda Zara 3a

When was the Talmud written?

The Talmud was not completed until the year 500 CE, but the task of writing down the Oral Torah began sometime after the year 70 CE after the destruction of the Second Temple in Jerusalem.

The Talmud states[122] that after the destruction of the Second Temple, the Jews were at risk of losing the Oral Torah, since it became increasingly difficult to study, teach and memorise the vast amount of knowledge.

Due to the persecution of the Jewish people, Jews were occupied merely with survival and rarely had the luxury of academic pursuits.

Moreover, even those who were able to study found it increasingly difficult to memorise the text, and pass it on in the oral format, as had been done for thousands of years.

Rabbi Yehuda Ha-Nasi (the sage known as Rebbe or "The Holy Rebbe") undertook the task of writing down the Mishna. This was not without controversy, many sages of the time felt it was against the ethos of Judaism, to write down any part of the oral tradition.

There were two main reasons why writing down the oral tradition was objectionable:

1. There is a law in Judaism which states: the written Torah may not be spoken orally, meaning one is forbidden from reciting a verse, without reading it from a written text. Likewise, the Oral Torah may not be written down, meaning one is forbidden from writing down any part of the oral tradition.
2. If the oral tradition were to be written, it would cease to be memorised, since one would no longer apply his/her full mental acuity to memorising the content, and could rely on the fact that they could always refer to the written text. This is similar to how

[122] Bava Metzia 85b

in the 21st century, we rely less on our memory and more on our digital devices to store information.

Despite these two major concerns however, it was decided that the Oral Torah had to be written down, since the alternative meant a complete loss of Jewish knowledge from the Jewish people, and the potential complete destruction of the Jewish nation.

They applied the verse[123]:

"A time to do for God, they abolished the Torah."

This meant that in order to preserve the Torah itself, a Jewish law had to be abolished, namely the law stating the Oral Torah may not be written down.

At first just the Mishna was written down, and later the Gemora, culminating in the works of the Babylonian Talmud.

There are several variants of the Babylonian Talmud. The oldest surviving manuscript dates back to 1342 and is known as Munich Talmud.

The first complete edition of the Babylonian Talmud was printed in Venice by Daniel Bomberg (1520–23). In addition to the Mishnah and Gemora, Bomberg's edition contained the commentaries of Rashi and Tosafos. Almost all printings since Bomberg have followed the same pagination. Bomberg's edition was considered relatively free of censorship.[124]

The Talmud which is considered the most textually accurate, and used as the standard version of the Talmud nowadays, is the "Vilna Shas" (Vilna Talmud).

[123] Psalms 119

[124] Amnon Raz-Krakotzkin. The Censor, the Editor, and the Text: The Catholic Church and the Shaping of the Jewish Canon in the Sixteenth Century. Trans. Jackie Feldman. Philadelphia: University of Pennsylvania Press, 2007. viii + 314 ISBN 978-0-8122-4011-5. p104

The Vilna Talmud was published by Menachem Romm of Vilna in 1835, and later on by his widow and brothers, of the Romm publishing house.

The Vilna Talmud like the Bomberg Talmud, contains the Mishna, Gemora and the commentaries of Rashi and Tosfos printed alongside each page. The page layout has remained unchanged for almost 200 years.

Other variants of the Talmud are not considered to be textually accurate but are studied by scholars, in addition to the standard Talmud.

There are also several methodologies of studying the Talmud. We will not discuss the methodologies here, as this warrants a discussion in its own right.

Why is the Talmud viewed with hostility?

As we mentioned above, the Talmud is viewed by some as inflammatory and discriminatory towards non-Jews. It is also viewed as being sexually deviant in nature.

The primary reason for this accusation is twofold:

Laziness:

Since the Talmud is so comprehensive and contains so much information, very few people are willing to spend the 20 or so years, reading the text.

Out of sheer laziness:

- Fabricated quotes are dished out in abundance.
- Quotes are taken out of context, with total disregard for the commentaries.
- Quotes are cherry-picked to suit a particular agenda.

As a general guideline, one should not quote the Talmud unless one has spent at least 20 years studying it, in depth and with its commentaries.

Hatred of Jews:

Any text can be twisted and distorted to support one's views, this is simply confirmation bias.

We look for information which supports our existing views, and we actively ignore any information which challenges our pre-existing views.

Even an innocent nursery rhyme; can be twisted and distorted to suit a particular set of values.

> As a general guideline, one should not quote the Talmud unless one has spent at least 20 years studying it, in depth and with its commentaries

Personally, I prefer an academic anti-Semite, to a lazy person who can't be bothered to invest the time and effort needed to understand a text.

I highly encourage Jew haters to study the text in detail. Anyone who has invested 20 years or more studying the Talmud and forms a hatred of Jews has earned his/her opinion. An educated opinion has value.

Eisenmenger and antisemitism

"No one is born hating another person because of the color of his skin, or his background, or his religion. People must learn to hate, and if they can learn to hate, they can be taught to love, for love comes more naturally to the human heart than its opposite."[125]

Nelson Mandela

The following is based upon a lecture given by Dr. Henry Abramson PhD, with several of my own observations, pertaining to this topic.

Dr. Abramson is an outstanding lecturer, who possesses profound and awe-striking knowledge of Jewish history, as well as being an exceptional Torah scholar. Dr. Abramson is one of those rare individuals who have mastered two worlds, the physical and the spiritual.

Personally, I believe he is a giant of the Twenty First Century, and would highly recommend his work (which is readily accessible) as a first port of call when studying Jewish history.

Despite Dr. Abramson's vast series of accomplishments, he carries an air of dignity and humility, which allows any person from any background to be fully immersed in his unique presentation.

Talmud animosity:

In the previous section, I discussed the Talmud, and stated that unless one has twenty years' experience studying the Talmud; one should refrain from quoting or criticising it. One can only appreciate what the Talmud is in the first place, after dedicating many years of intense Talmudic study.

To this end, my favorite anti-Semite would be none other than Johann Andreas Eisenmenger, the author of a two-volume, two thousand page

[125] Long walk to freedom: the autobiography of Nelson Mandela, Nelson Mandela - Little, Brown - 1994

book written in German called "Entdecktes Judenthum" (Judaism Unmasked/Uncovered) which gives a scathing account of Judaism.

Eisenmenger rips Judaism to shreds, and is considered by some as the father of modern-day anti-Semitism. Adolf Hitler was greatly inspired by the works of Eisenmenger, and one could say that Mein Kampf is a "watered down" version of Eisenmenger's work.

You may be wondering, why an orthodox Jew would call the biggest anti-Semite his favourite anti-Semite. The answer is simple: Eisenmenger was not a lazy fool, blurting out second-hand anti-Jewish rant, he spent twenty or so years studying the Talmud, and he is therefore entitled to form an opinion, an opinion is earned through study.

All anti-Semites should follow in the way of Eisenmenger. First study and understand, and only afterwards form your own unique opinion about Jews. As a Jew, I would rather be hated by someone with a valid opinion, than an ignorant fool. If anti-Semitism entailed lifelong study, and spiritual awakening, I would be pro anti-Semitism, because one who understands Judaism will find nothing to hate.

The life and works of Eisenmenger[126]:

Eisenmenger was born in 1654 in Heidelberg and received a good formal education. As a student Eisenmenger studied to become what is termed an "Orientalist", a term not widely used today.

An Orientalist was one who studied the languages, and culture of Hebrew, Aramaic and Arabic. Eisenmenger mastered these languages, and had a passion in particular for understanding the Hebrew and Aramaic texts.

Eisenmenger pursued his academic career, and studied in several institutions including in his hometown of Heidelberg, as well as in England.

Eisenmenger himself writes, about a life-changing incident: as a young man, Eisenmenger heard a rabbi giving a sermon. The rabbi, being

[126] Johann Andreas Eisenmenger. (2016, September 28). In Wikipedia, The Free Encyclopedia

unaware there were non-Jews present at his sermon, began to criticise Christians. The Rabbi's criticism of Christians was highly offensive to the young Eisenmenger.

Moreover, Eisenmenger was later appalled to learn about three Christians who had converted to Judaism.

This event and possibly others led him down the path of understanding Judaism, as an insider but from a Christian perspective.

Eisenmenger conducted a field anthropological study of Judaism. His mission was essentially to understand Judaism fully, and to ensure no Christian would ever consider the possibility of converting to Judaism.

Posing as a "would-be" convert to Judaism, Eisenmenger studied Judaism for 19 years, both at Heidelberg and Frankfort am Main. He studied the entire Talmud several times, and even formed close relationships with prominent Jewish authorities.

Eisenmenger, became fully integrated into the European Jewish community, marrying a Jewish woman, and raising Jewish children.

In his 2000 page work, published in the year 1699, Eisenmenger quotes 182 Hebrew books, 13 Yiddish books and 8 works by non-Jews. His work is a comprehensive, scholarly and academic dissertation, of noteworthy proportions.

As Dr. Abramson notes, the word "anti-Semitism" is actually grammatically incorrect. There is no such word as "Semitism".

The very word "Semitism" was created by Wilhelm Marr in the 1880's. The word "Semitism" referred to what we would call "Globalism".

This was the idea, that there was a group of Jews who secretly wanted to control the world. The concept of a group of people wanting to control the world was called "Semitism".

Marr was "anti" "globalism", and the term used to express opposition to globalism was antisemitism.

Thus a term was created to replace the common word in German "Judenhass" meaning "Jew-Hatred" and the true word is "antisemitism", a single word, which is more politically correct.

Antisemitism is simply a way to express hatred of Jews using academic terminology.

Antisemitism a fight against globalism:

While it may or may not be true, that there does exist a group of people who want to control world events, few if any would be Jews.

Moreover, if there were to be few Jews, found within these circles, they have no desire to advance a Jewish agenda.

In fact, the very opposite is true, the Jews involved in such movements, are extremely hostile to faithful Jews who believe in the Creator.

The small percentages of atheistic Jews who have this goal, are embarrassed by their Judaism, and would readily eradicate practicing Jews in their millions, given the first opportunity. A globalist agenda has absolutely nothing to do with Judaism.

To call the "Globalists" Jews, is absolutely ridiculous, as globalists hate Jews more than any other group of people. The absurdity is reminiscent of medieval antisemitism.

Therefore to call a small group of "Jews" within the remaining part of a group which support globalism, a "Jewish Group" is entirely misrepresentative. Thus Wilhelm Marr was partially correct but distorted the facts.

Jews have been hijacked:

Jews have been hijacked, in this sense. As Jean-Paul Sartre (1945) wrote in his essay: Réflexions sur la question juive, "Reflections on the Jewish Question"[127], if there was no Jew, the anti-Semite would have invented him.

From the medieval period, Jews have been used as a scapegoat for all of the world's problems. Even the spread of bubonic plague was blamed on the Jews. It wasn't until many innocent Jewish people were slaughtered, did the peoples of Europe conclude that killing Jews, was not the remedy.

Not much has changed since then, and today as in all periods in history Jews are blamed for globalism and its ill-planned consequences.

If you are reading this text, you can help to spread the word that the Globalists used Judaism as a front, for their agenda, knowing full well it would be easy to get away with any crime, by blaming it on the Jews, it's the oldest trick in the "playbook".

Real Jews practice Judaism, not Zionism, communism or capitalism. Since so many individuals are willing to believe half-truths, and have neither the time nor desire to study the matter fully, they almost always come to the wrong conclusion. Sometimes half-truths are worse than outright lies.

It is very sad that real Jews, i.e. those who wish to serve the Creator, and practice Judaism, are grouped together with the very people who want to replace and destroy Judaism.

[127] December 1945 in Les Temps modernes

Antisemitism in various forms:

As Dr. Abramson discusses there are four unique stages or periods of antisemitism.

1. **Xenophobia** - a Greek term meaning "fear of strangers".

The ancient civilisations had animosity towards Jews based on a misunderstanding of Jewish differences.

The ancients felt that Jews were not religious, since they did not participate in the common cultural practices of the day. For example if the ancient Greeks held a large orgy, in honor of a pagan god, Jews of that period would be unlikely to attend.

This would be viewed by the ancient Greeks as being "unpatriotic" and "non-religious". The Greeks would assume that Jews had no god, since they did not participate.

Jews were also considered to be lazy and slothful in the early Roman period. Since Romans had very few public holidays, the average Roman would work almost 365 days a year. Jews on the other hand didn't work every Saturday.

Thus misunderstandings based on observed behavior, caused friction and animosity. This early period was not as intense and not specifically aimed towards Jews, but towards any culture that did not fit the norm.

2. Early Christian anti-Judaism:

The second period marks a distinct move, from generalised misunderstandings to specific hatred towards Jews.

This started with early Christians who were banned from the Jewish synagogue. Those who believed that Jesus was the Messiah were expelled from the synagogue.

John, the author of the gospel[128], was Jewish and was forcibly removed from the synagogue, as he held the belief that Jesus was the Messiah.

Early Christianity had to distinguish itself from its parent religion of Judaism. In fact early Christianity was indistinguishable from Judaism, barring one element, namely the belief in Jesus as the Messiah held by Christians, and the belief that Jesus was not the Messiah held by Jews since he had died.

Therefore in order to elevate Christianity, Judaism had to be lowered. Rosemary Radford Ruether (1974) writes antisemitism is the left hand of Christology[129]. There is a mother-daughter relationship between Christianity and Judaism.

Thus in order for Christianity to be elevated and distinguished, Judaism had to be lowered. This period of antisemitism was more hostile and aggressive.

3. Medieval antisemitism:

During the medieval period, hatred of Jews went beyond all forms of rationality. Even the popes of that period often protested to the form of antisemitism which was taking place.

Many strange and bizarre claims were made about Jews, which were entirely ludicrous. Addressing an illiterate and uneducated audience, would often be the key to win support for anti-Jewish activities.

---

[128] Gospel of John. (2017, January 23). In Wikipedia, The Free Encyclopedia

[129] Rosemary Radford Ruether (1936-) (Grant D. Miller Francisco, 1999)

Some of these beliefs included:

- It was the belief that Jews drank the blood of non-Jewish children, which has absolutely no basis in Judaism. This is the era of the "Blood Libel".
- It was believed Jewish men had horns like the Devil, and would thus cover their heads.
- It was believed that Jewish men had menstrual periods like women.
- It was believed illness and diseases were caused by coming into contact with a Jew, such as was the case with the outbreak of bubonic plague.
- It was believed that Jewish women would lay eggs, and not give birth to living offspring.

These bizarre ideas were mainly spread due to the lack of power Christianity felt. As the powers of church and government separated, the need arose to undermine Judaism so that all religions would have no value within society.

4. Modern antisemitism:

Modern antisemitism focuses on two aspects, namely:

A. Racism
B. Conspiracy

The modern anti-Semitic stance is that Judaism is racist, or that Judaism is a race which is impure, and requires genetic intervention to help maintain a pure human race.

Eugenics:

Starting from the 1800s it was widely believed that various races of human beings were inferior to others. These "faults" in the human genome were studied closely in the hope of eradicating the faulty genes responsible for genetic mutations which resulted in human abnormalities.

The eugenics program reached great heights under the reign of Adolf Hitler where the sub-humans could be eradicated in order to purify the human gene pool.

The following were some of those considered to carry sub-human genes:

1. The mentality retarded
2. Blacks
3. Jews
4. Homosexuals

The modern form of antisemitism allows for Jews to be eradicated in the name of eugenics and racial purity. This is well portrayed in the film Der Ewige Jude[130] (The Eternal Jew 1940).

Some lay a different claim saying that Jews, do not mix with non-Jews and are thus preserving their own race, while being hypocritical of white supremacists. The question of whether Judaism is a race will be discussed in another section.

Conspiracy:

The second form of modern antisemitism revolves around conspiracy theories. Although the world is abundant with lies, cover-ups, corruption and conspiracies, not all of the above are attributed to the Jews.

Whether UFOs are Jewish flying control devices, or whether Abraham Lincoln and John F. Kennedy were killed by the same Jew, needs further analysis.

What is a conspiracy?

The word conspiracy has its roots in the word conspire. There are two elements in a conspiracy namely:

1. The grouping of individuals (i.e. individuals forming a group)
2. The desire or plan to do harm (the plan is usually secretive)

[130] Deutsche Film Gesellschaft, Fritz Hippler, 1940

Used in a sentence we could say the following:

"Six men are conspiring (planning in secret) to rob the local bank"

There is no doubt that the six men and the local bank exist, their plan is the conspiracy.

Every conspiracy theory can be validated, and either accepted or rejected. In fact any theory if properly constructed can be tested with the null hypothesis.

The only hindrance to testing a conspiracy theory is that the information is hidden and secretive. Therefore conspiracy theories are not some dogmatic belief system, in which you chose to believe or not, theories are subjected to testing.

The idiot-proof method:

In order to form and hold a valid opinion about any topic, especially one that concerns the nature of the universe or the human condition, one needs to have the following skills:

1. The ability to **think critically** (i.e. to falsify your own beliefs)

2. A working knowledge of **research methodology**, in the social sciences.

    - Collecting information from multiple and opposing sources, for example.
    - Forming a hypothesis and null hypothesis.
    - Testing the theory using valid research methods of theory testing.

3. A working knowledge of analytics and **philosophical reasoning**:

- Knowing the difference between deduction and induction, for example.
- Knowing the difference between a premise and a conclusion.
- Knowing how to spot flawed reasoning, such as "call to authority", "straw-man" etc.

Any person, who has these three skills, can investigate and form a valid opinion, provided that enough time and energy are invested in the pursuit of the truth. Conversely, any person, who lacks these skills, will undoubtedly form incorrect conclusions, and sow misinformation.

Sharing an opinion is equivalent to sharing a condom:

In order to form a valid opinion about a topic, a great deal of effort is needed. Each person can form his/her own unique opinion based upon his/her own research. You need to be the owner of your opinion.

Sharing an opinion is equivalent to sharing a condom

However, to hold an opinion based on the opinion of another individual is what I call "opinion sharing" and sharing an opinion is the equivalent to sharing a condom.

Fake news and post-truth:

The year 2016, gave birth to two new concepts, which bear testament to the stupidity of the masses.

In our modern society, laziness and lack of education have created a generation of people who are unable to discern information on their own. Like the illiterate Europeans of the medieval period, today we have illiterate thinkers who believe anything and everything.

Any person, who collects information from one source, has broken the first rule of research methodology. Thus any person, who gains his/her, views and beliefs based solely on legacy media would have never stood a chance of obtaining truthful information.

Likewise any person, who collects information solely from alternative media sources, also has no chance of obtaining truthful information.

Truthful information can only be obtained by collecting information from multiple and opposing sources.

"Fake news" and "post-truth" are terms used to distract uneducated people who lack the three critical skills needed.

Just as the illiterate people of the 1700's did not understand the concepts of money and banking, and were thus left in the dark, and readily exploited, owing to their lack of knowledge. So too are modern day individuals readily exploitable if they lack the knowledge and research skills.

Only in a world of confusion and lack of understanding can exploitation occur.

The lazy option:

Rather than sharing an opinion or condom, those who desire to know the truth about any topic, but are unable or unwilling to spend the many years of research required to form valid opinions, have another asset at their disposal.

If one wants to know the truth about any topic simply follow the money trail.

Although this method is not entirely scientific, following the money trail by asking:

1. Who benefits financially?
2. What are the financial benefits?

Following the money trail, will often yield more accurate results, than years of scientific research.

In conclusion: With dedicated and scientific research all conspiracies can be known in full. Laziness on the other hand begets hatred, and allows people to share condoms, and opinions.

- The Talmud is a collection of the Jewish oral tradition. There is nothing sinister about the Talmud.
- Even for Eisenmenger, who spent the required time and effort to form a valid opinion, has just that, an opinion not fact.
- One who shares Eisenmenger's opinion without personal research cannot be taken seriously.
- Eisenmenger had a personal agenda and was subject to confirmation bias.
- Only those with a pre-existing hatred of Jews will conclude that the Talmud is sinister or discriminating.

14

KHAZARIAN JEWS

The Jewish State of Khazaria:

When one thinks of a modern-day Jewish state, many people automatically think of Israel. However from the year 650 to 1048, a period of more than 400 years, a Jewish state existed in the heart of modern-day Eastern Europe and Asia, called Khazaria.

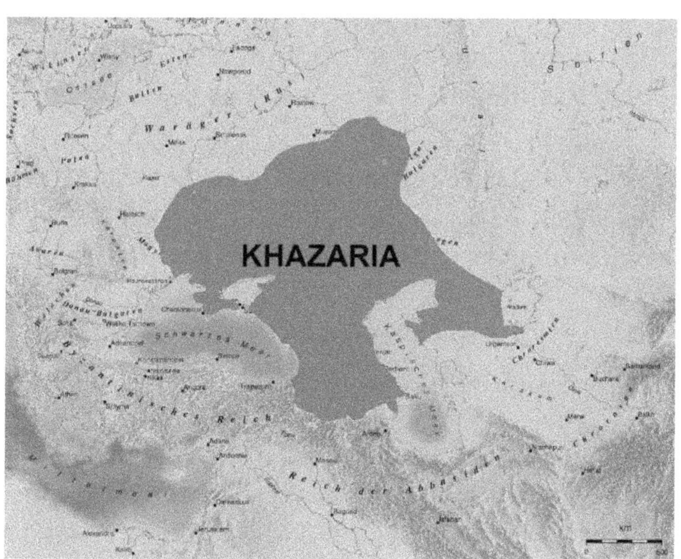

Khazaria was an exceptionally large state[131] with its borders reaching:

- North - modern-day Samara in Russia.
- South - modern-day Van in Turkey.
- West - modern-day Kiev in the Ukraine.
- East - modern-day Nukus in Uzbekistan.

The history of Khazaria:

The history surrounding the formation of the Jewish state of Khazaria, is not exceptionally well-documented. There are several studies however detailing some key events during this period.

The kingdom of Khazaria, was situated in a very strategic location.

To the north and east of Khazaria, the population was predominantly Christian, whereas to the south and west, the population was predominately Muslim.

Relations between Christians and Muslims during this period were hostile, and thus trade between the east and west as well as between the north and south, would have been hampered due to the religious and political ideological differences between these two regions.

King Bulan[132] realised his region was at the epicenter of a major clash of cultures. It is said that King Bulan set about on a mission, to learn more about the three Abrahamic faiths: Judaism, Christianity and Islam.

Fearing an invasion of his territory by either Christians, or Muslims, King Bulan decided to adopt Judaism as the official religion of Khazaria.

Whether this state-wide conversion was sincere, or merely a way to create a neutral territory as a trading route is not known for certain.

[131] Ten times larger, than the modern state of Israel.

[132] The History of the Jewish Khazars, Douglas M. Dunlop, Princeton, N.J.: Princeton University Press, 1954

However, the state-wide conversion was adopted as official law, with all Khazarian citizens undergoing a full rabbinic Orthodox conversion to Judaism.

Thus starting with King Bulan, all the residents of this vast territory became Jewish, forming the largest Jewish state in modern history.

Controversies surrounding Khazaria:

There are several controversies surrounding the Jewish state of Khazaria. Some maintain that the conversions were not sincere, and were merely a political tool used for trading purposes. However evidence found in the "Cairo Genizah" has revealed the Jews of Khazaria did in fact practice Orthodox Judaism[133].

The fact remains however that the adoption of Judaism did support trade between Christian and Muslim countries, as both were happy to trade with the Jewish state of Khazaria. Khazaria thus became a buffer zone, or proxy for trade between Christian and Muslim countries.

Some maintain that King Bulan was a Khagan; that his people were war-like in nature, and somewhat uncontrollable, and he thus sought to govern his barbaric like people, with the rules and regulations found within the religion of his choosing.

In all likelihood, there were some citizens who adhered to the state religion of Judaism, as a patriotic act, and thus practiced Judaism in its entirety, while others merely followed the rules of the country, and were not entirely affiliated with any religion.

In recent times, the issues surrounding this topic have resurfaced. I therefore feel that it is necessary to remove this obstacle, for those that are in search of the Creator.

This is a sensitive topic, and it has been used as a basis for Jew hatred. Naturally I am inclined to defend my people, and as such I would like to dispel the myths surrounding this politically charged topic.

---

[133] Dr. Henry Abramson PHD

Are Ashkenazi Jews descendants of the Khazarians?

There are two primary issues which give rise to the questions below:

A. "Are Ashkenazi Jews descendants of Khazarians"
B. "Are Khazarians sincere converts?"

The questions above are based upon two primary factors namely:

1. Observed behavior of Ashkenazi Jews
2. DNA testing: Does the modern-day Ashkenazi Jew share common DNA with Khazarians or with Middle Eastern Jews?

I would like to dispel the myths surrounding this politically charged topic

Observed behaviour of Ashkenazi Jews:

In order to understand this issue we need to understand the biblical account of the "Givonim" people, in the days of Joshua.

When Joshua conquered the land of Ca'naan (biblical Israel) approximately 3000 years ago; the land of Ca'naan was not vacant but occupied by seven different tribes of Ca'naani people known as[134]:

1. The Chiti
2. The Emori
3. The Ca'naani
4. The Prizi
5. The Chivi
6. The Yevusi
7. The Givoni

Joshua was ordered to give these seven tribes, who were the local inhabitants of the land of Ca'naan, three options:

[134] Joshua 9:1

1. Stay in Ca'naan and fight for their territory.
2. Leave their land, and settle elsewhere.
3. Stay in their land, but be observant of the Jewish laws applicable to them.

The vast majority of Ca'naani people chose the first option, and decided to stay and fight with the Israelites. Over a period spanning approximately 14 years, each Ca'naani tribe, lost in battle to the Israelites, and subsequently lost their land.

The Givoni people (Gevonim in plural), did not wish to be killed in battle. In addition, they did not want to vacate their land, nor did they want to accept or be governed by Jewish law.

The Givoni people came up with an alternative solution to the crises which their people faced.

Since Joshua was only commanded to fight with the seven Ca'naani nations, and not with any other group of people, the Gevonim disguised themselves as nomads not affiliated to any group.

The verses in Joshua tell the account of how the Gevonim went about deceiving Joshua[135]. The Gevonim dressed themselves in worn out clothes and shoes, rode on emaciated donkeys and carried stale bread among other things.

When they encountered the Israelites, they said "We have come from a faraway land...." "Please make a promise to us that you will not harm us..." and so on.

Joshua gave them the benefit of the doubt, despite the Israelites insistence that these people were imposters.

Joshua had made an oath in the name of God that he would not do any harm to this group of people.

[135] Joshua 9:3-27

Subsequently, Joshua found out that he had been deceived, and that these "nomads" were in fact the tribe of Gevonim.

Joshua was faced with a dilemma; on the one hand he had been deceived, and should have killed the Gevoni people. On the other hand, Joshua had made an oath in the name of God that he would do no harm to this group of people.

Joshua then decided that since he could not kill the Givoni people, as this would be a violation of his oath, and since he was also obligated to banish this group of people, he would make the Givoni people "slaves" instead.

The Givoni people were assigned the functional tasks of being woodchoppers and water carriers[136] for temple services.

The commentaries[137] explain that Joshua wanted the Givoni people, to be surrounded by the Kohanim (priests) of the temple service, in order for them to learn from the ways of the Kohanim, and in turn become better and more refined individuals.

Thus their slavery was not so much about humiliation, but rather about training and learning about Jewish culture and ethics, albeit as slaves.

The Givoni people continued to live among the Jewish population for more than 300 years, with a large population of Givonim, living in the city of "Nov".

"Nov" was a city dedicated to priests, and was something of a training camp for Jewish priests to learn the temple service, in great detail. The priests of the city of "Nov" supported the Givoni people by way of financial and material assistance. The city of "Nov" was a tranquil place, something akin to a city dedicated to meditation and prayer. Its residences were in line with living an esoteric lifestyle, removed from physical pursuits.

[136] Joshua 9:27
[137] Me'am Loez ibid

The city of Nov:

As described earlier, Nov was a priestly city, a city devoted to the service of God. As such, Nov had little to no defenses.

At the height of animosity between King Saul, the first Jewish king and David, his son-in-law, Saul embarked on a nationwide manhunt, to find and kill David.

One of the most tragic events in Jewish history was the destruction of the city of Nov, known as the City of Priests.

The story is recounted in the book of Samuel[138]: when King Saul was in pursuit of David, it was said that David was hiding in Nov.

Eager to capture and kill David, King Saul laid waste to Nov the city of Priests. The verses state that on a single day, 85 priests were killed.

Not only was this a great atrocity in the sense, that many innocent lives were lost, it was a very tragic event in the sense that the men killed, were priests, people who were of the highest spiritual standing, and this was a huge loss for the Jewish people.

The Givonim seek revenge:

Approximately 300 years after the story of Joshua, in the days of King David, there was a famine which had lasted for three years.

The story is recounted in the book of Samuel[139], the famine was retribution for the atrocities committed against the Givonim.

The Givonim, had a grudge against King Saul, and in retribution, they wanted seven of King Saul's relatives to be killed.

---

[138] Samuel 1 Chapter 22 verses 17-22

[139] Samuel 2 Chapter 21 verses 1-12

Rashi[140] offers two explanations as to why the Givonim wanted seven of King Saul's relatives to be killed:

1. When King Saul invaded Nov the city of Priests, seven Givonim were killed. These included: two woodchoppers, two water carriers, an attendant, a singer and a scribe. Thus King Saul was responsible for the death of seven Givoni men.

2. When King Saul invaded Nov, and killed all the priests, the Givonim lost their income and sustenance. Since the Givonim were reliant on the priests for their income, King Saul's actions of killing the priests had an indirect consequence of causing the Givonim to lose their income. Someone who causes another to lose their income is considered a murderer. Thus King Saul was considered a murderer for having caused the Givonim to lose their income.

The verse states[141]:

"And the Givonim were not of the children of Israel….."

Rashi explains this verse based on the Talmud which states[142], that there are three qualities present in a Jew, namely:

1. They are merciful.
2. They are ashamed (when doing something inappropriate).
3. They do acts of kindness.

Although the Givonim had the right to bear a grudge, against King Saul, they acted in a manner of cruelty nevertheless, by requesting that seven of King Saul's relatives be executed.

[140] Rabbi Shlomo ben Yitzack on Chapter 21 verses 1 and 2 ibid

[141] Samuel 2 Chapter 21:2

[142] Yevamos 79a

Thus the verse is elaborating that, even if the Givonim converted to Judaism, they were not considered by God to be Jewish, since they lacked the compassion needed to be considered a Jew.
One who is a Jew will have the three aforementioned character traits, and one who does not possess these traits, does not descend from the children of Israel.

The argument based on observed behaviour:

Some maintain that Ashkenazi Jews have difficulty expressing emotions, such as empathy, warmth and compassion.

This observed behaviour is circumstantial, as it is based on subjective observations, as well as the observer's personal experiences. Furthermore, it does not place a specific origin on the said group of people.

In addition it is worthy to note that statistically speaking Ashkenazi Jews have the highest IQ amongst several groups tested in the world[143]. It is not uncommon for those with high IQ's, to be less functional in the emotional domain[144]. Thus the observed bahaviour may simply be the result of an imbalance between logical and emotional intelligence. Therefore this argument is purely speculative at best.

In conclusion to the observed behaviour argument:

To state categorically, that Ashkenazi Jews are Khazarians, is false.

Today Ashkenazic Jews have become intermingled. There are Ashkenazi Jews, who are in actual fact Sephardic in origin, such as Lithuanian Jews, who are in actual fact migrants from Spain. There are also Sephardic Jews who have lost their heritage and follow the laws and customs of Ashkenazi Jews. Thus dividing sub-categories of Jews is mostly irrelevant.

---

[143] Cochran, G., Hardy, J. and Harpending, H., 2006. "Natural history of Ashkenazi [intelligence." Journal of Biosocial Science, 38(5), pp.659–693.

[144] Such as people suffering from Asperger's syndrome

The only conclusion one can draw with certainty, is that any individual who claims to be of Jewish descent, or who claims to be Jewish, but lacks the three aforementioned character traits, has questionable descent, and may not be Jewish in actual fact.

A person with questionable descent is not necessarily a Khazarian, but may originate from any group of people.

The argument based on DNA:

The second argument was made popular by the writer Arthur Koestler in his book titled The Thirteenth Tribe[145]. Koestler asserts a theory which states Ashkenazi Jews are not the descendants of the biblical Israelites, but are rather the descendants of the Khazars. One of the primary goals of Koestler was to assert that the Jewish people are not a race, and should therefore not be subjected to racism.

In more recent times geneticists have studied the DNA markers found within Ashkenazi Jews. Their findings show predominately that Ashkenazi Jews share genetic markers indicating they share similar ancestry to the Jews of the Middle East.

To understand this argument fully, one needs to bear in mind that males have X and Y chromosomes, while females have two Y chromosomes. Since Judaism is passed on, through the maternal bloodline, only markers on mitochondrial DNA or mtDNA would be of any relevance[146].

Dr. Jon Entine, in his book Abraham's Children[147] demonstrates that until the year 1600 there was an average population of only 50,000 Ashkenazi Jews in Europe. The majority of Jews in the world were Sephardic.

[145] The Thirteenth Tribe, Arthur Koestler, United Kingdom, Hutchinson, 1976
[146] Mitochondrial DNA is passed on from mother to daughter.
[147] Abraham's children: race, identity and the DNA of the chosen, Jon Entine - Grand Central - 2008

Entine notes, that the conversion of Khazars to Judaism was limited to the nobility of Khazaria, meaning only noblemen and noblewomen converted to Judaism, while the majority of the population did not.

Genetic markers show that modern-day Ashkenazi Levite Jews have a very strong linkage to Khazarians. His theory proposes that since Khazarian noblemen wanted to be considered the "upper class" in their new religion of Judaism, they wanted to be Kohanim (Priests); the highest tier of Judaism. However this was not possible since only paternal descendants of Aaron the Kohen, could be Kohanim. Thus as a "consolation prize", Khazarian converts of noble ancestry were awarded the second tier status of being a Levite.

Another observation made by Entine, was that there is a strong linkage in the ancestry of the "Kohen Gene" (the priestly gene) handed down from father to son.

An important genetic discovery:

The biggest and most noteworthy observation of Entine; is that most European Jews do not share Middle Eastern ancestry on their maternal side. He found that European Ashkenazi Jews, had paternal genetics, linking them to the Middle East, but maternal genetics linking them to the local population.

This would suggest that Ashkenazi European men, married local European women, who may or may not have converted to Judaism.

Since Judaism is passed on, through one's mother, genetics would indicate that European Ashkenazi Jews are predominantly of European descent.

Other genetic research:

When one examines the issue to the question:

"Are modern-day Ashkenazi Jews, descendants of the Khazarians, and unrelated to the Israelites of the Bible?"

One will note that there are in fact two questions rolled into one.

1. Are modern-day Ashkenazi Jews descendants of the Khazarians?
2. Are Ashkenazi Jews related to the Israelites of the Bible?

These two questions are independent of one another. If Ashkenazi Jews are not related to the Israelites of the bible, this does not automatically mean Ashkenazi Jews are related to the Khazarians.

Each question has to be studied independently, and one may find that Ashkenazi Jews, are not related to the Israelites of the Bible, nor are they related to the Khazarians.

When one examines this topic, one will find two schools of thought:

- Those who do not ascribe to the "Khazar Theory" and maintain that Ashkenazi Jews of today are not descendants from the Khazarian people. Researchers in this category include: M.F Hammer et al[148] and Almut Nebel et al[149] among others.

- Those who do ascribe to the "Khazar Theory" and maintain that Ashkenazi Jews of today are descendants of the Khazarian people. Researchers in this category include: Eran Elhaik[150] and Arthur Koestler[151] among others.

When examining this issue, one will note that those who are, both for and against the theory are propelled by a political agenda.

---

[148] Proceedings of the National Academy of Sciences, Jewish and Middle Eastern non-Jewish populations share a common pool of Y-chromosome biallelic haplotypes M. F. Hammer, 2000

[149] Nebel, A., Filon, D., Brinkmann, B., Majumder, P. P., Faerman, M., & Oppenheim, A. (2001). The Y Chromosome Pool of Jews as Part of the Genetic Landscape of the Middle East. The American Journal of Human Genetics, 69(5), 1095-1112.

[150] Elhaik, E. (2009). The compositional organization of mammalian genomes: characteristics and evolution

[151] Koestler, A. (1976). The thirteenth tribe. United Kingdom: Hutchinson

Some would like to state that all Jews form part of a race, in order to further their agenda of collective Jewish hatred. Typically these individuals are against the "Khazar Theory". Others would like to hate specific groups of Jews and these individuals are for the "Khazar Theory".

In reality however, this issue is politically charged, and for the purposes of searching for the Creator, one can steer clear of this issue and focus only on that which is pertinent.

One can be certain of several facts in this regard:

1. Firstly - we have no genetic material of the Khazar people in question; therefore we lack any comparative sample. Unlike the DNA tests at the scene of a homicide, where we have samples of DNA from both the victim and the suspect, in this case we only have the DNA from one party.

2. Genetic tests, such as the one in question, can tell us very little about the group in relation to other groups. All genetic tests can tell us in this instance, is where in the world a group of people originate from.

In this genetic research, all we have is group testing. This means we can test particular chromosomes, and say with a high degree of certainty, where these genes emanate from geographically.

3. Studies which show paternal linkage are not relevant in terms of Jewish law, since the bloodline of Judaism is passed on through the maternal ancestry.

4. Paternal linkage is useful only as far as priesthood is concerned, since the status of a Kohen (priest) is passed on through the paternal ancestry. Priesthood only becomes a relevant topic once the Jewish status has been confirmed. Establishing a maternal

linkage in ancestry would thus have to precede any examination into paternal ancestral linkages.

5. Although numerous studies have been conducted by all races, religions and ethnicities around the world regarding this subject, this topic is too politically charged. Therefore one can be speculative of all findings by all researchers.

In conclusion:

Without doubt, there are many people in the world today, who are in fact Jewish, and who have no idea. Likewise there are many people in the world today, who are not in fact Jewish, but who practice Judaism.

The amount of intermarriage and lost records over the centuries would make it almost impossible for anyone to prove with absolute certainty whether they are Jewish or not. Thus one has to rely on the limited information at one's disposal.

There are many people in the world today, who are in fact Jewish, and who have no idea.

If one has an ancestry, of several maternal generations, being observant Jews, one can safely assume that one is a Jew. One who believes that they are Jewish should investigate.

Two types of worlds:

The Ramchal writes the following[152]:

The world can exist in two states:

1. "The true optimum state of the world exists when man grasps the path of wisdom and is engaged in devotion to his Creator. In such a world, truth is obvious and unambiguous. Bad is prosecuted and subjugated, and deception no longer exists...As a result of this, security and tranquility prevail, and there is no longer any pain and suffering or injury. The Creator openly projects His glory on such a world..."

2. "The opposite of this optimum world exists when man becomes overwhelmed by the pursuit of physical desires, rejecting wisdom and furthering himself from it. Truth is ignored, bad is reinforced and prevails, and deception and error increase. It is a world of false values, where good qualities are eclipsed and bad qualities prevail. As a result of this, tranquility ceases to exist and there is no security, whilst there is much suffering and injury..."

It should be quite clear that we have chosen state number two, and that we need to alter the course of history, should we wish to prevent pain and suffering.

[152] The way of God: (Part 2 Providence / 8. Details of providence)

In every thought, speech and action, question whether you have done so for the sake of the Creator.

1. **Source has made every being with love and kindness for the benefit of all.**

   The Creator has not just made rocks, plants, animals and human beings but every being which exists. The Creator is concerned with the development and well-being, of everything, because everything belongs to the Creator. The Creator wants all beings to benefit, from creation.

2. **Attach yourself strongly to the Creator and you will remember all that you know.**

   Your primary objective, and the reason you were entrusted with life, is for you to attach yourself to the Creator by means of self-improvement. Your Soul was given a briefing as to how and what you need to do; you already know what you need to do, and you need to "Remember" that which you already know. By making a strong connection to your Creator, you will attain ever-deeper levels of understanding. You have a soul within you to guide you.

3. **Strengthen yourself, in order that we may all, be attached to our one Creator.**

   Improve yourself and become the best person that you can be - physically, emotionally and spiritually. The more fully-functional human beings there are, the more the human race can assist one another. If every human being is no longer burdened by mundane tasks, we can all focus our time and energy on attaching ourselves single-mindedly to the one Creator.

4. **Together, let us seek unity of the Creator as our only goal.**

   By collaborating in a unified effort without undermining one another, or coercing one another, we can be one, just as our Creator is one. When the human race works in unity on any project, success is guaranteed. The ultimate goal is for humanity to recognise the Creator.

5. **Be subservient to nothing other than the Creator of all.**

   Since all beings, regardless of their greatness, are subservient to the Creator, one need only subjugate one's will to the Creator and not to human beings or deities. Be true to yourself, live your life together with the Creator.

6. **Your greatness is only the manifestation of the Creator.**

   All greatness that you see stems from the will of the Creator. No being can accomplish any task without the Creator, and one must thus recognise the source from which greatness comes.

7. **Emulate only the Creator the one of love and kindness.**

   Just as the Creator created all beings with love and with kindness, so too one must emulate the Creator, by developing oneself into a selfless being, one who is compassionate and kind-hearted.

8. **Take away only what you can replace, and only for the sake of the Creator.**

   Do not take the life of an individual[153] unless you are able to restore it. Since human beings and other beings are prone to mistakes, always think before you act. If you are certain that your action is correct, ensure that you are doing so for the sake of your Creator, and not for selfish purposes.

9. **Have mercy on all entities, in order for the Creator to show mercy to you.**

   Whatever thought, speech or action you make, do so with mercy. Have positive thoughts towards others, speak gently to others, and act kindly towards others. Even when one is compelled to do that which is seen as cruel, one should act in a manner that displays mercy. Thus, one should not torment other beings; for just as you have power over that which is beneath you, so too are there powers above you, who may act likewise.

10. **From one began all existence and to one it will return.**

    Just as the Creator started the process of existence so too will the Creator end existence, for anything which has a beginning must have an end. All that exists will be reabsorbed back into the Creator from whence it came.

Anything which has a beginning must have an end

[153] See page 224 – There are many deeds which constitute murder. Ones actions can cause another to die, on an emotional and spiritual level, without it being noticeable on the physical level.

There was one, there is one and there will be one.

We have now explored the doctrine of peace to be understood on the simplest level. Deeper understanding can be attained with each subsequent reading.

Creator of all worlds, may it be your will that you reveal your presence to us, and may we accomplish all that we have been tasked to do, in all incarnations. May we merit to rise and merit in the world to come. May all our actions be pleasing to you, for we have no abilities and in you we trust.

We give gratitude to you for remembering your covenant

ברוך המקום ברוך הוא ברוך שומר הבטחתו

הַבֵּט מִשָּׁמַיִם וּרְאֵה
כִּי הָיִינוּ לַעַג וָקֶלֶס בַּגּוֹיִם
נֶחְשַׁבְנוּ כַּצֹּאן לַטֶּבַח יוּבָל
לַהֲרוֹג וּלְאַבֵּד
וּלְמַכָּה וּלְחֶרְפָּה

וּבְכָל זֹאת שִׁמְךָ לֹא שָׁכָחְנוּ. נָא אַל תִּשְׁכָּחֵנוּ

ותגער בשטן לבל ישטינני ויהי נא דלוגנו עליך אהבה

www.ingramcontent.com/pod-product-compliance
Lightning Source LLC
Chambersburg PA
CBHW062039090426
42740CB00016B/2954
* 9 7 8 0 6 9 2 0 7 1 5 1 9 *